Best wishes from
Paul Clarke

JUN5 1999

NEVER SAY NEVER

Couran Cove Resort • From Dream to Reality

Ron Clarke

Photography by Leo Meier

The Couran Cove Resort Environmental Research Trust

With thanks to Chuck

ENDPAPERS: *The intricate leaf venation of Macaranga tanarius, one of the many rainforest species encountered on site.*

FRONT COVER: *Twenty kilometres of pristine ocean beach, a most superb run on firm, even sand.*

FRONT COVER INSET: *The elevated boardwalk, through the dense rainforest, is built of recycled timbers.*

PAGE 1: *The graceful tree frog (Litoria gracilenta) can be heard calling during the warmer nights of the year.*

PAGES 2–3: *Eucalypt woodland is prevalent throughout the property.*

PAGE 4: *A curious agile wallaby (Macropus agilis) seen hiding in thick sedgeland.*

PAGE 5: *A developing flower of the saw-leaf banksia (Banksia serrata) is one of the most common species on the estate.*

PAGES 6–7: *Gum Tree Point which overlooks the Marine Resort.*

PAGE 8 (THIS PAGE): *The majestic forest red gum (Eucalyptus tereticornis) is the dominant tree on site.*

PAGE 9: *The Marine Apartments present some interesting geometric angles.*

PAGE 10: *The huge leaf of the cabbage-tree palm (Livistona australis).*

PAGE 12–13: *Clayton's Lake, a freshwater lake on the eastern foreshore, is a window into the island's vast watertable.*

Published by
The Banyan Tree Creative Services
exclusively for
The Couran Cove Resort
Environmental Research Trust

© 1999 The Couran Cove Resort Environmental Research Trust

© Photographs Leo Meier/CCRERT

All rights reserved. No part of this publication may be reproduced, stored in or introduced into a retrieval system, or transmitted, in any form or by any means (electronic, mechanical, photocopying, recording or otherwise), without the prior written permission of the publisher.

National Library of Australia Cataloguing-in-Publication data

Clarke, Ron, 1937- .
Never say never : Couran Cove Resort from dream to reality.

Includes index.

ISBN 0 9585729 5 X.

1. Couran Cove Resort. 2. Resorts - Environmental aspects - Queensland - South Stradbroke Island. 3. Resorts - Queensland - South Stradbroke Island - Planning. I. Title.

333.78099432

Created and produced by Cecille Weldon
Photography: Leo Meier
Design: Stan Lamond, Lamond Art & Design
Editor: Vicki Barclay
Creative consultant: Bruce Perry
Printed and bound by Jade Productions

Contents

14
Introduction

22
The Place of Our Dreams

56
The Island and its History

80
Getting Started

106
Protecting the Environment

138
Bringing it all Together

168
Living the Dream

190
Index

Introduction

Ron Clarke

The nectar-filled flowers of coastal banksia (Banksia integrifolia) attract birds and bats by the thousands.

'You can never retain environmental purity and develop a large resort,' we were told. 'It's impossible to overcome the acid sulfate soils that are so dominant in the site without enormous, unviable costs being incurred,' they said. 'The experience of Hamilton Island has shown the barging costs to get building materials to an island are such that the end product becomes too expensive to be competitive,' the experts told us. 'The indigenous Aborigines will never let you build, and if they don't interfere with your plans, the conservationists and the environmentalists will,' was the most common comment.

NEVER SAY NEVER!

One of the many nocturnal inhabitants encountered on a night's walk. OPPOSITE: A Kites Nest Eco-Cabin glimpsed through the surrounding bush.

Throughout my life I have never been impressed by anyone who told me that something or other was not possible.

Would you believe that when I started in athletics in 1953 the general wisdom was that the human body could never run a mile faster than 4 minutes, or 3 miles faster than 13 minutes, nor 6 miles faster than 27 minutes? It wasn't long before the first sub-four-minute mile by Roger Bannister opened the floodgates of sub-four-minute milers. (More

The verandahs of the Eco-Cabins, screened from insects and the sun, offer cosy retreats.

than 500 athletes had achieved this feat by the end of 1997.) I personally took great satisfaction in being the first to prove the fallacy of the latter two claims.

The Couran Cove Resort site is the most unique environmentally packed site in Australia—it has everything. Every type of bushland in the country (except desert) is represented within its boundaries, from mangroves to rainforest, it's there.

This variety of flora brings with it a similar diversity of wildlife—butterflies, birds, frogs, small animals of all kinds—the Resort teems with activity.

The challenge of developing a Resort that does justice to this jewel of Australian bushland was a thrilling one. We had to harness environmental groups and use their expertise; we needed to design appropriate buildings that blended into the landscape and were made from materials which enhanced their setting; and we wanted to create systems to preserve, protect and even enhance (dare I say it) the pristine beauty of the site.

This is the story of how the Couran Cove Resort team set new standards for the construction of a Resort anywhere, inventing, discovering, innovating and assisting nature in our mission to create a holiday destination the like of which cannot be matched.

From our earliest days we adopted the motto AS NATURE WOULD HAVE IT.

'When I surged only Michel remained.' Ron Clarke at the World Games, Helsinki in 1965.

OPPOSITE: Tree ferns (Cyathea cooperi), uncommon on site due to past burning practices, are being regenerated in the Resort's Native Plant Nursery.

Introduction

Couran Cove Resort is exactly, or soon will be, as nature would want it to be. Guests and visitors are continually amazed at the wonder of their surroundings.

For the real hero is South Stradbroke Island itself.

As can be seen from the variety and majesty of Leo Meier's magnificent photography there is nothing but infinite variety in the sights and sounds that abound on the island.

These pages will whet your appetite, just as the Resort will stir the soul of every true Australian. For all the beauty illustrated herein, nothing equals the real thing. Come and see us yourself. The reality is far more spectacular than even I dreamed it could be.

A foraging agile wallaby (Macropus agilis) on the western Broadwater beach at sunrise.

OPPOSITE: *The sand, like an artist's canvas of footprints, is returned to a blank by an incoming tide.*

FOLLOWING PAGES: *Sunset through the mangroves at low tide.*

The Place of Our Dreams

Ron Clarke

Helen and Ron Clarke enjoying a typical summer holiday at the beach.

I recall that it was the Melbourne summer of 1987-88. Helen, Nic and I were back in our home town visiting our other two children, Marcus and Monique. ABC Radio invited me in to chat with Caroline Jones and she asked me where my favourite spot in the world was.

We had been living in London and Bath since leaving Australia early in 1983 and had travelled extensively in Europe and northern America for the past 30 years. But I suppose we all tend to savour our early days and despite all the wonderful places we had seen and experienced, I had no hesitation in nominating not one, but two spots in Victoria that I had always cherished. The first was the beaches of Port Phillip Bay. Maybe they are not all that dramatic in either scenery or surf but from my earliest days I loved the beach.

A soldier crab (Mictyris sp.) *forages for organic material from the sand.*
OPPOSITE: *A flock of terns faces into the prevailing south-easterly.*

A grove of horsetail oaks (Casuarina equisetifolia) *perched above the eastern foreshore.*

We grew up in Essendon, on the north side of the Yarra River, and the only time we ventured south was to visit the Junction Oval when St Kilda was playing Essendon on their home ground, or to go to the beach. And those were very special days that we anticipated for weeks. Usually they took the form of a club picnic.

My father was a born organiser. He was always doing things for people—Union Steward, Cricket Club Secretary, Football Club Social Secretary. He would organise dances, theatre parties, outings and, above all, picnics. Some were to the hills, usually to a property called Rob Roy at Christmas Hills where small Shetland ponies were bred, or to the beach, normally Chelsea. Furniture vans were booked (with parallel seating knee to knee), every family brought their food, thermos flasks for tea, rugs, picnic plates and so on. The ground and the tables were booked 12 months ahead. Pick-up points around the city were arranged with an early start so we would be at the beach by midmorning. Straight after lunch came the races—sack, 3-legged, flag, wheelbarrow (you held your partner's legs while he 'ran with his hands'), rolling-pin throws and the inevitable game of beach cricket or football. Home at dusk with a singalong on the way back early into the evening. They were great days.

Then there were our Christmas holidays. From the time I was six or seven years old we always went to Hindhope Park on Boneo Road, Rosebud. The Mornington Peninsula was Melbourne's poor man's Riviera, with the wealthy Toorak 'snobs' (as we used to think of them

Ron's father, Tom Clarke was a footballer for Essendon in the 1930s.

OPPOSITE: **The grey mangrove (Avicennia marina) plays a valuable role in binding the sand of the Broadwater and providing a nursery environment for marine life.**

at the time) lazing about in their summer houses at Portsea, then back towards Melbourne were the beaches of Sorrento, Rye, Blairgowrie, Rosebud, Dromana, Mt Martha, Mornington, Mt Eliza and Frankston (the end of the suburban railway system, where we all had to catch huge trailer buses). We used to go down there for two weeks just after Christmas. All our New Year's Eves were at Hindhope Park until I was 16 years old, after which we went to my aunt's who had a beach house at Dromana instead.

I didn't know it at the time but my future wife Helen was having exactly the same sort of experience, but at Dromana the adjoining beach to Rosebud, at the same time each year. She and her family stayed at a smaller guesthouse, Mana Lodge, which had a similar set-up.

Ron and his brother Jack building sandcastles at Rosebud.

Hindhope Park had around 75 cabins, bedrooms really, with each 25 being allocated a separate kitchen and adjoining dining facility. Every family had their own wood-fired stove in the community kitchen and their own table, pantry cupboard and icebox (no refrigerators in those days, nor television) in the adjoining common dining hall. The camp managers kept firewood supplied and dishes were washed in the sinks surrounding the stoves.

Every evening there was a different social function, organised by my father of course—old-time dance, mixed dance, concert, fancy-dress ball and so on. All the kids were entertained beforehand with a variety of games and competitions.

The Place of Our Dreams

The music for the dances was played on a single piano, by the same bald-headed pleasant lanky man called Charlie, who always dressed in a black suit and looked like an undertaker with a smile. He kept rhythm with his left foot which banged away in perfect harmony on the wooden floor eliminating the need for any percussion instruments.

Then there were the sports days, the tennis tournaments, the tug-o-wars and fishing contests—the late night wading in the shallows with little spears and lights attached, trying to separate the shape of a flounder from the background of the sand, which camouflaged the fish perfectly. The only way to spot them was to see a pair of tiny eyes, or a little tuft of sand when a nervous fish twitched slightly on our approach. We were told to spear them between the eyes (so as not to mess up the flesh you understand) but to us anywhere was good enough. We missed a lot more than we speared as the fish seemed to sense they had been spotted and shot away so quickly.

The foreshores were full of campers with their tents and caravans, sited cheek by jowl, making it almost impossible to find a pathway between them to the beach. Families booked the same site for the same time each year through generations, and they still do.

Judges happily camped next to garbage collectors or wharf labourers—I love the Australian informality which conquers any notions of social strata—in this country you are who you are and not what you are.

FOLLOWING PAGES: South Stradbroke Island boasts one of the best beach breaks for surfing on the Gold Coast.

A healthy diet of shellfish keeps the wading birds in top condition, the results of their last meal seen on the shore.

We spent all day on the beach paddling canoes, playing cricket, racing through the shallows, building sandcastles, swimming, talking and generally fooling around. There was always a Fair at which you would waste your money, or a putt-putt golf course or bounceball (singles volleyball on a trampoline) of which we would have innumerable contests.

I think it was probably those wonderful days which ensured that the beach always meant so much to me.

Later Helen and I had our first home on the small mountain called Arthur's Seat which overlooked both Dromana and Rosebud. As a matter of fact we spent our honeymoon there doing it up. It was a choice between going interstate and spending the cash, or adding the money to our house deposit. As Helen's parents wouldn't agree to her being married unless we had our own home, we opted for the latter and spent an idyllic couple of weeks doing the garden etc., with our two dogs—a German shepherd (Baron Storm) and a miniature dachshund (Colonel Pewter), completely broke.

As we grew more affluent (a few years and a couple of babies later), we moved back into the outskirts of Melbourne, at the foothills of the Dandenongs to a little suburb called Heathmont. Our lovely three-level house was built in and around an old quarry with some huge eucalypts on the site which blended beautifully with the wooden house. It was here that my running career was suddenly resurrected. Then, when we became even more affluent, moved to Brighton—one of the suburban beaches of Melbourne's 'Golden Mile'.

The large and robust form of the coastal banksia (Banksia integrifolia) make it ideal for pollination by birds and small mammals.

OPPOSITE: *The name 'Couran' was an original Aboriginal name for one of the larger gum trees, Moreton Bay ash (Eucalyptus tessellaris), on site.*

33

The Place of Our Dreams

OPPOSITE: **Coastal banksia (Banksia integrifolia)** will grow in dense forest, but here it must stretch and reach for the light.

The laughing kookaburra (Dacelo novaeguineae) is the largest of our kingfishers and can be found in a variety of habitats.

Ron, Helen and their three children in 1970. Marcus is on Ron's back, baby Nicolas in his arms, together with Monique.

It was whilst we lived at Heathmont that I was introduced to my other favourite spot—the Dandenongs and especially the national park.

I had been induced back into running and taken to the grass tracks of the Caulfield Racecourse as a place to train on my way home from work. I was Head Office Accountant of Lamson Paragon Limited, a large Australia-wide business form printing group. Their offices were on the Boulevard at Richmond, overlooking the Yarra River. It was a superb location. I didn't have to deviate too far from my direct route to Heathmont to drop into Caulfield and this I did each night after work. It was there that I met up with a marvellous bunch of runners in their early 20s (I was 24 at the time) from the Glenhuntly Club.

Soon we were all improving on our times for the distance events, so what started as a 'get-fit' hobby began to become more and more important to me. My friends, Tony Cook, Trevor Vincent, John Coyle, Rod Bonella and I thrived on the routine and they introduced me to Ferny Creek, where the house of clubmate Frank McMahon was the base for their Sunday morning 20-milers. I joined them and, thereafter, this became an integral part of my week—whatever we did the previous night, wherever we competed on the Saturday afternoon, we always turned up for the Ferny Creek Run the following morning. I kept it going for 20 years (until I began having problems with the mitral valve in my heart as a result of the Mexico City Olympic fiasco), even after we had shifted to Brighton which added a further 20 kilometres onto the journey to get there.

The Place of Our Dreams

I do not have the slightest doubt that these runs along the paths around Ferny Creek, amongst the giant mountain ash and eucalypts, were absolutely the singlemost important influence in my subsequent running career. Had I not gone there and done that I would not have won a single Australian title. The restfulness, the purity of the air, the beauty of the surrounds, combined to strengthen and, at the same time, relax both body and mind so that each Sunday morning became almost a religious experience.

And so I just could not separate these two magical spots, so full of memories and enchantment, when asked by Caroline to name my world bests.

On 14 October 1995, we returned to Australia to build Couran Cove Resort. In March 1998 I was asked the same question by a journalist who was writing an article for the *Australian Women's Weekly*. He, in fact, interviewed me for some 30 minutes over the telephone and he asked me to name my favourite place in Australia and why. I immediately thought back to my response to Caroline Jones 10 years earlier and although by then I had seen a lot more of Europe than I had in 1988, I still remembered Rosebud and Ferny Creek vividly. Nevertheless, I had

FOLLOWING PAGES: *Paperbarks (Melaleuca quinquenervia) reach for the top.*

Ron on one of his many Ferny Creek runs. 'Happiness is running with my mates around me in the hills.'

The Place of Our Dreams

changed my mind. I had been introduced to South Stradbroke Island. Consequently, I had no hesitation in nominating South Straddie. Why?

Because it has everything. It combines Rosebud and Ferny Creek and adds in the most perfect expanse of ocean surf beach that can been seen anywhere, a breathtaking cabbage-tree palm-dominated rainforest, and a peacefulness and serenity that can only be experienced on an island thousands of miles away from civilisation.

What follows is how we have been able to take this little piece of paradise and convert it lovingly into the most wonderful Resort in the world.

Ever since I started to travel overseas I had begun to play mind games about the 'perfect place'—my dream land. I would be enchanted by little English villages, or the Norwegian mountains, the Swedish lakes, the Austrian valleys and the Swiss vistas. I have loved London and Paris and Vienna and Rome. We spent a delicious week at Nice. I cannot recall a country we didn't like and our favourite game was to imagine building a resort or a hotel at various sites that we saw.

But who would want to live away from Australia?

The food in this country, the 'feel' of the place, the friendliness and lack of pretentiousness of its people is just so good; perhaps unappreciated fully until you leave it all behind and go overseas for a while. But five years away from Australia and you really miss it, after 10 years the yearning to come home becomes an obsession. Memories of the place recur more and more regularly. When the opportunity finally came we could not believe our luck.

OPPOSITE: *A rich understorey of juvenile cabbage-tree palms* (Livistona australis) *forms an imposing barrier.*

Cabbage-tree palms (Livistona australis) *take many years to develop a trunk, as can be seen from the size of this juvenile.*

Combe Grove Manor, that Helen and Ron Clarke lovingly restored, had a magnificent garden with 2,000 roses.

Whilst we were in Europe we had the opportunity to completely refurbish and rebuild an old manor house, Combe Grove (built circa 1712 in Bath), into a Country Club Hotel. Helen redecorated every square inch of the main house, whilst we retained all the facades of the old stables and outbuildings but pulled down the interiors to construct all the sports club facilities—gymnasiums, changing rooms, aerobics studios, swimming pools, etc. The gardens we also did over completely taking them back to their former glory of the 19th century. We engaged Bill Mount, a delightful man who is a landscape gardener specialising in historical reconstructions.

Bill, with Helen's encouragement, returned Combe Grove Manor to its glory days as well. We opened the Club to the locals as a sports facility and, in no time, had 2,500 members. The small hotel section (45 beautiful suites) flourished as well, especially as we built a great little hideaway Conference Centre. We both enjoyed the experience thoroughly whilst still maintaining control over our London Health and Fitness Club, Cannons, which continued to exceed expectations, and budgets.

Certainly we relished the challenge, so the opportunity to develop South Stradbroke was doubly welcome because we had gone through it all before in one of the most charming places in England—the manor house had 55-mile views over the rolling hills and valleys to the south of Bath right through until the White Horse at Westbury.

OPPOSITE: *The versatile swamp oak (Casuarina glauca) reaches tall heights in the competitive rainforest environment, but here on the beach is much smaller.*

The Place of Our Dreams

OPPOSITE: Melaleuca is a Greek derivation for 'black and white', referring to the tree's appearance after a fire.

A developing flower spike of the coastal banksia (Banksia integrifolia).

Interpacific Resorts (Australia) Pty Ltd was established in 1989 when the Interpacific Group (IPG) purchased the freehold of 60 hectares from our current neighbour Bruce Small. Bruce retained a much smaller holding around his own resort. This is a small but attractive day-visit facility and he is busy developing a residential village alongside with 85 sites.

IPG planned to build a Pacific Island Club in Australia. Their Pacific Island Club brand had been doing very well in the Pacific rim countries, especially in Saipan, Guam and Phuket. They also had established the Bali Country Club in 1993 at Nusa Dua. The Pacific Island Clubs cater mainly for tourists from neighbouring countries, especially Japan, and provide them with a type of Club Mediterranean that is most popular.

However, with the recession of the early 1990s, a decision was made to shelve, then later to cancel, their plans for South Stradbroke Island. In fact, some tentative feelers were put out for potential buyers. The Queensland Government was asked if they would make a swap for mainland sites in view of their interest to preserve the whole of the island as an environmental park.

I cannot describe my emotions when I first set foot on the site there. It had been a wet Christmas and I have to admit I did not have high expectations (being an ignorant Southerner, I had never heard of South Stradbroke Island until I was

A Macaranga tanarius seedling punches through the leaf litter on the rainforest floor.

The Place of Our Dreams

asked to have a look at it on our next trip home). Underfoot it was a little squelchy but as we made our way across the property from the Broadwater we were spellbound by its beauty. Helen is a little chary about the bush and spent most of the visit on the lookout for snakes in the undergrowth (they terrify her) but the majesty of the trees and the teeming wildlife overwhelmed even her. It was late afternoon and the wallabies were everywhere, and then we came to the surf beach—wow—rolling surf and beautiful white sand bordered by wandering sand dunes as far as the eye could see in both directions.

This was the place of our dreams—as Australian as the slouch hat.

It encapsulates virtually every kind of vegetation you will find in Australia in just one single property. There are the Mangroves on the western side bordering the Broadwater; then the Rainforest, the Melaleuca Swamp, the Natural Bush and the Sand Dunes. These are covered in more detail later in the book by our Environmental Team who are much more expert than I am in describing their various characteristics. All I knew was that this was Ferny Creek and Rosebud all wrapped up together with some rainforest and the best surf beach I had ever seen thrown in.

What a site for a Resort!

The agile wallaby (Macropus agilis) is a rapidly disappearing species on the mainland but is abundant on South Stradbroke Island.
FOLLOWING PAGES: *The rolling sands on the eastern foreshore are stabilised by tufts of grass and sedge.*

The Place of Our Dreams

Its location, just a dropkick off the mainland coast, is perfect as it does not have the accessibility problems of the other islands such as Dunk, Hamilton, Great Keppel and Hayman. Just a 15-minute ferry trip out of Runaway Bay, which in turn is but 40 minutes from either Brisbane or Coolangatta airports, the Resort would be within a 3-hour journey of anywhere in Australia bar the far West. You could leave home in Melbourne at 6.00 am and be having brunch overlooking the rolling surf at Couran Cove Resort by 10.00 am—almost quicker than driving from Melbourne to Portsea during those summer holidays.

Pigface (Carpobrotus glaucescens) *is a succulent dune creeper which provides not only this lovely flower, but also a delicious red fruit.*

The closeness to the mainland also means that all the theme parks, the restaurants, golf courses and shopping centres that proliferate along the Gold Coast are also within easy reach. Yet once on the island a feeling of complete isolation engulfs you—life immediately becomes less stressful—the sand and the surf take over the psyche.

So here we were with the opportunity of a lifetime—two lifetimes. We sat back in our hotel room at Sanctuary Cove and talked for hours. By the next morning we had the bones of a plan mapped out—by the end of that day, everything seemed clear. We phoned our close friends, Kay and Daryl Jackson at their beach house at Bermagui and described what we had seen and the type of resort we thought would work there. We asked Daryl if he could sketch out some ideas of buildings and apartments and, as usual, he came up with the perfect designs.

OPPOSITE: **The moving contrast between development and isolation, as the eye looks south over Clayton's Lake towards Surfers Paradise.**

Daryl and I had been friends since we sat side by side in a desk overlooking the Essendon Football Ground in 6th grade at Essendon State School. Our unforgettable teacher, an elderly Austrian called Henry Stielow, had a system of classifying students as to their ability starting with those who needed most help in the front rows, gradually working through to the back rows and across to the windows overlooking the ground.

We sat in the second back desk immediately adjacent to the windows. I was on the window side and Daryl was on my right. The trouble was, Daryl is an over-the-top left hander which meant he sat to the left of his school book whilst his arm looped over the top of the paper and his wrist was completely the wrong way around. As a consequence he took up about two-thirds of the seat whilst my quite large backside had to fit onto the remaining 6 or 7 inches (15 or 17½ cm). Despite this constant clashing of arms and behinds we remained good friends through the ages. Daryl married Kay Parsons who was at Essendon High School with Helen and me (Daryl went to Wesley College, one of the private schools in Melbourne). He and I were Captain and Vice Captain of the Essendon Football Club's Under-19 Team (known as the Thirds), and we played against each other in the Mornington Peninsula League (he with Sorrento, me with Hastings).

I looked after his financial records and his tax, when he first started in business in Melbourne with a partner, Evan Walker, that I also knew from school

Essendon State School, 1947. Ron Clarke (far right, middle row) and Daryl Jackson (second left, back row) in the premier football team. The successful teamwork continues to this day.

days—this time from Melbourne High (where we both matriculated in Form 6A3). I even visited Daryl and Kay regularly on my athletic trips overseas as Daryl moved around the world studying under various famous architects. I remember spending a couple of days with them in a freezing little flat in New Haven where Daryl was studying under Professor Rudolph at Yale. It was snowing and icy and I tried running outdoors, finding it utterly impossible and highly dangerous—I slipped on black ice every time I got up a decent speed.

When I first went to England I had turned to Daryl to redesign Cannons, our London Health and Fitness Club, as the English architects kept coming up with plans I considered unimaginative, uninspired and boring. In one hour Daryl had sketched out a concept which was exactly right. I persuaded him to open a London office and he has been responsible for all the vitality and freshness Cannons still portrays and communicates to its members.

It is not by idle chance it is the most successful Club in Europe, if not the world, with 10,500 members in the City Club; 5,400 at Covent Garden (another Jackson design) and in excess of 25,000 member visits each week.

Daryl came through once again with plans and layouts for the Resort that fitted in with our ideas perfectly.

As the Resort developed it reflected almost exactly these early pencilled plans. The series of A3 sketch sheets Daryl sent up for us to look at were the most exciting things I had ever seen. I could see it all happening, I could imagine the magnitude, yet the simplicity of it all—the possibilities to

Early morning dew in the heart of the rainforest.

The Place of Our Dreams

provide a Resort the like of which had never been seen before. One that would allow families to get away from it all and have a really simple old-fashioned holiday full of activity and relaxation, as complete a break from the stress of earning a living as they could ever attain.

I admit Couran Cove Resort is designed for Australian families. Australians are unique in their lack of pomposity. They could not give a damn about who they are sharing their holidays with as long as they behave themselves and 'don't come the raw prawn'. I wanted a place without social barriers, that kids from all backgrounds, and all ages, no matter their creed, colour, politics or wealth, could play together, enjoy themselves and, above all, relax. No concrete jungles or creepy-crawlies (the human type), no nightclubs or four-wheel-drive vehicles, no noise, no crime and no drama—just holidays as they used to be.

You could not achieve this on the mainland. You cannot get it on most islands and you certainly couldn't get it overseas.

Here was the place. This was the property I never thought existed. I had discovered my dream and I was about to be given the chance to live it.

FOLLOWING PAGES: *An impenetrable wall of leaves and stems marks the boundary of the rainforest.*

OPPOSITE: *Saw-leaf banksia (Banksia serrata) is well adapted to fire with a thick, corky bark for protection.*

The delicate, scented flowers of Moreton Bay ash (Eucalyptus tessellaris).

The Island and its History

Lindy Salter

Rainbow lorikeets (Trichoglossus haematodus) frequent Couran Cove when there is an abundant supply of nectar from flowering trees.

Traditional owners

It is thought that Moreton, North Stradbroke and South Stradbroke islands were once joined, forming a long narrow peninsula beginning at the Southport Spit. This gave easy access to mainland Aboriginal people visiting the island tribes. Archaeological studies have confirmed continuous Aboriginal occupation of the islands from the Pleistocene age.

Tribes of Aboriginal people using the island included the Noonuckle (northern North Stradbroke), the Goenpul (southern North Stradbroke and northern South Stradbroke), the Quandamooka (the bay islands) and the Kombamerri (southern South Stradbroke and the mainland, south of Coomera River). Their occupation of the island was nomadic and completely in harmony with nature.

Juvenile coastal banksia (Banksia integrifolia) possess serrated leaves to deter potential grazers, then develop entire leaves as they mature.

Their affinity with nature was demonstrated by their use of dolphins to herd shoals of fish towards shore for easy netting and their use of natural signs to forecast the seasons. They knew that large numbers of 'blue mountain parrots' (rainbow lorikeets)

Low tide reveals the footprints and feastings of some of South Stradbroke's marine and estuarine creatures.

in autumn meant a good season of mullet would follow, whilst an abundant flowering of wattles told them the mullet would soon be plentiful.

Mainland tribes would have visited from time to time—for social interaction and a change of diet, especially seafood feasts. A present-day elder from the Kombamerri people recalls his grandmother describing trips to the southern end of the island, and walking up to North Stradbroke to visit friends and relations. Middens (mounds of shells of edible molluscs), which can still be found on the island, are evidence of these gatherings. The limited extent of archaeological remains suggests the middens were temporary transit camps en route between the coast, the river valleys and the mountains to the west. (The island was at that time part of the mainland.) A survey in 1963-64 located 28 of these 'kitchen sites' on South Stradbroke Island. Relics found then included flaked stone artefacts, bones and charcoal.

The strength and obvious good health of these people, as noted by early white observers, was probably due to the quality of natural food on the island. Fish, shellfish and other seafood were supplemented by turtles, wallabies, snakes, lizards, echidnas and bandicoots. Flour was made by grinding the roasted fern root (bungwall) into a powder before making a type of damper. Honey was obtained from the flowers of the banksia as well as from nests of native bees. Berries and fruit were plentiful. Fishing nets were made from the bark of the native cottonwood tree and dilly bags from the cabbage-tree palms and beach spinifex.

The large broad leaves of the cabbage-tree palm (Livistona australis) are ideal for catching light in the competitive rainforest environment.

OPPOSITE: *Coastal banksia (Banksia integrifolia) produce an abundant supply of large flowers from summer through to winter.*

The kangaroo apple (Solanum aviculare) is one of the fast growing native tobaccos found in Australia.

OPPOSITE: Beach spinifex (Spinifex sericeus) and sedge (Isolepis nodosa) work together to bind the moving sand on the eastern foreshore.

The grey mangrove was used to make shields, whilst boomerangs came from the prickly stemmed tree called a jeerabing, as well as the roots of the cypress pine. The local people bartered with mainland tribes for knives, axes, grindstones and spears.

South Stradbroke became a separate island in 1898 when wild seas broke through the narrow sand isthmus at Jumpinpin.

Steak and Oysters

'As a horse breeding station—NOTHING EXCELS CURRIGEE'

Thus read an advertisement offering the Currigee Run for sale in 1880. The southern point of the island, Moondarewa, was first used by graziers who swam cattle and horses across from Southport. Although it was never a prosperous venture, some cattle remained on the island until 1971, when they were removed because of damage being done to revegetation work.

Before the breakthrough at Jumpinpin in 1898, when North and South Stradbroke were one island.

Oysters were once so plentiful in the sheltered waters of Moreton Bay that they were burned for lime to make cement. Some builders thought live oysters gave the cement more body. Fortunately the residents of Brisbane appreciated their gourmet value, and one of the early Acts of the Queensland Parliament was the Oyster Act—which prohibited this practice and introduced oyster leases.

The Island and its History

The town of Currigee had its origins as the southern base for the Moreton Bay Oyster Company which was formed in 1876. Small oysters (culture) were brought from other parts of the bay to the growing banks at Currigee. The 'once-famous Currigee' was described by Thomas Welsby as 'a cosmopolitan village, with coloured people of various nations, and a few white, mainly employers'. Local residents recall families of Aboriginal, Swedish, Chinese and English origins at Currigee. Today, the one remaining grave at Currigee bears the remains of Ben Manager, the infant son of one of the oystermen, who died in 1890.

Once a base for fishermen and oystering, Couran was subdivided into small farms in the 1920s. Unlike the sand elsewhere on the island, the soil at Couran was rich and loamy. Several families took up the land but struggled to make a living over the next 20 years. One of the farmers, Bob Latter, arrived as a teenager and purchased an 80-acre (32-hectare) block and a boat for £95 ($190). The land was mainly forest and mangrove swamp which first had to be cleared and drained. Bob dug a channel through the swamp with a timber walkway beside it to allow access by boat. Unpredictably high tides covered his crops one year (around 1948) and Bob abandoned the farm soon afterwards.

Oystering at Rat Island opposite South Stradbroke.

FOLLOWING PAGES: *The grey mangrove (Avicennia marina) protects the western beach from erosion.*

The grave of little Ben Manager, who died at Currigee in 1890, is still there today.

An elder of the Kombamerri people tells us that 'Couran' is an Aboriginal word for Moreton Bay ash. Other meanings from tribes nearby were 'eldest brother' or 'dugong skirt' (as in steak). Early maps show Cooran and Quaran as alternate spellings.

Families of fishermen had also established themselves on the island as anyone with a fishing or oystering licence could squat on adjoining land. They fished from large open boats with three pairs of oars, and an optional sail, often pulling their nets as far as Moreton Island. Boats would race each other to the Brisbane or Southport markets. During the Depression it was not uncommon to go to Southport for the cheque, only to be handed a bill instead. Fish which were not sold had to be dumped—and the fishermen paid the bill!

Forest, much of which remains today, on Stradbroke Island in 1889.

Whisky and Dynamite

Some visitors to the island arrived unexpectedly—when their ships were wrecked on the island's shores. Currigee people featured in two such events. The *Scottish Prince* came to grief on the Southport Bar in 1887, without loss of life. Thomas Welsby observed:

'As for the men of Currigee, what a time they did have . . . I verily believe cases upon cases of spirits were "apprehended" by the willing and energetic worker, and that to this day many a plant lies hidden on the shores of Stradbroke.'

OPPOSITE: **Evidence of burning, such as scars on the trees and many species regenerating in open patches, can be found throughout the rainforest.**

The Island and its History

In 1894 the *Cambus Wallace* was wrecked near Jumpinpin. A sailor swam ashore and raised the alarm. However this time police and customs officers supervised the salvage, and Welsby described it as 'more of a temperance picnic to many when compared to … the *Scottish Prince*'. The cargo contained large quantities of dynamite which was later ignited. The explosion caused a large crater to form in the sandhills, and many believe this contributed to the breakthrough which occurred four years later.

Holidays

The appeal of the island to amateur fishermen and picnickers has always been strong. As early as 1897, Richard Gardner, a Southport grazier, publican and pilot, offered:

'Pleasure trips to Stradbroke. The new steam launch, *Southport*, will make trips from Nerang Creek Heads and the Grand Hotel to Stradbroke on Sunday (7.3.1897). First trip 9 a.m. … Return fare 1s.'

The Tuesley and Lyons families were others who recognised the tourist potential of the island. They built sheltersheds, shops and houses at Moondarewa and ran regular ferry trips across. In 1957, Lachie Tuesley leased some land at Tuleen, and took boatloads of tourists there for barbecues and picnics.

Campers at Stradbroke Island, Christmas 1885, escaping the throngs on the mainland.

OPPOSITE: *Another day, another beautiful sunset on the Broadwater.*

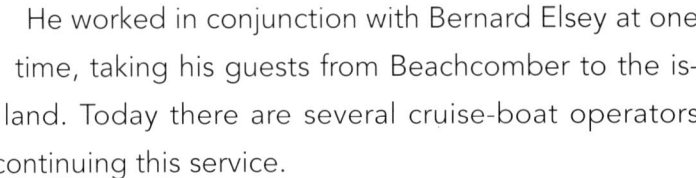

He worked in conjunction with Bernard Elsey at one time, taking his guests from Beachcomber to the island. Today there are several cruise-boat operators continuing this service.

The first holiday establishment on the island was Roe's Kamp. It was founded at Moondarewa by Reginald Roe, an early headmaster of the Brisbane Grammar School. Boarders from the school who were unable to go home in the holidays, accompanied the Roes to the island. The Kamp was moved up to Picnic Point when the land eroded in 1938, and remains in the family's hands to this day.

On several occasions, the island has caught the eye of developers—keen to expand the glitz of Surfers Paradise. In the late 1950s the Hooker-Rex company planned to build a bridge to the island near Currigee, and to develop all the remaining Crown Land. The plan included sites for a hospital, parks, churches, hotels, schools, a golf course and a heliport. Fortunately, the scheme was thwarted by sandmining companies who would not relinquish their leases.

A canal development was first proposed for Couran in 1967. Approximately 100 hectares (250 acres) of old farmland was acquired by Colin Steeley who planned a $55,000 Boatel. The canals were constructed, and the first of 72 Samoan-type huts were erected. The others remained on the mainland when the company folded.

The Hooker-Rex plans in the late 1950s were modelled on a development in Florida. The sandmining companies would not relinquish their leases and the project folded.

The Island and its History

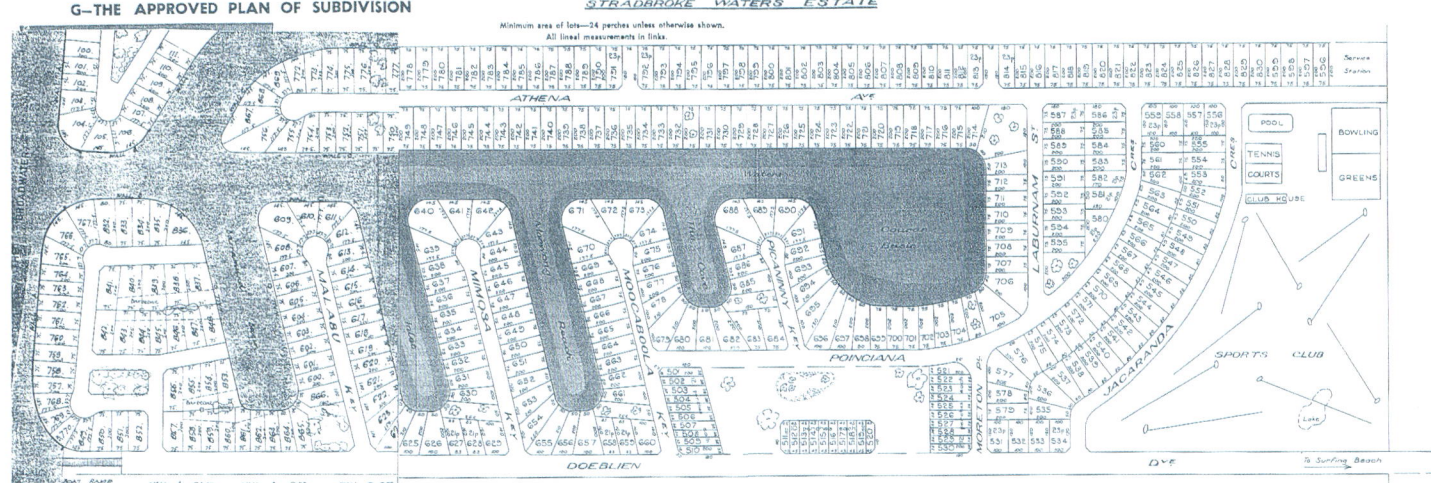

The Couran land has changed hands several times since then. Today, Interpacific Resorts owns the northern section and has developed the eco-tourist resort, Couran Cove.

This development was like many on the Gold Coast but did not proceed.

The tavern at Tipplers began operations in 1972. Now known as the South Stradbroke Island Resort, it boasts a restaurant, fast food service, beer garden, sporting facilities and 40 burees for guest accommodation—all set in 4 hectares of lush tropical gardens.

Shifting Sands

An awareness of the fragile nature of this sand island began with its constant erosion and was heightened by the presence of sandmining operations. Mineral sands

Sandmining on the beach, in the 1950s and '60s, probably slowed development on the island.

were extracted during the 1950s and '60s. Restoration efforts were commenced by the mining company and assisted by the Beach Protection Authority which began a research station on the island in 1971. Their presence, and the removal of the cattle, has largely succeeded in stabilising the once mobile dunes. Broad areas of former wasteland now boast a healthy cover of wattles, casuarinas and banksias. The Research Station closed in 1998, leaving their buildings and some equipment for the use of the Gold Coast City Council. The construction of the Southport Seaway in 1984 has now stabilised the southern end of the island.

Nature's School

The first use of the island for educational purposes was probably by Reginald Roe. (It's hard to imagine a 19th-century schoolmaster not wanting to share his knowledge of the island with his schoolboy visitors.) Currigee had a large enough population to apply for its own school in 1890. A one-teacher school operated in the town for 16 years. Mainland schools have long seen the value of the island as an educational resource. Day trips and camps are frequently organised, and the Southport School has a permanent camp site at Dux's Mooring. Education Queensland has an Environmental Education Centre at Jacob's Well which brings parties of school children to the island on day trips and camps. Primary and secondary school children are able to study the history and ecology of the island first-hand.

A dragonfly perches delicately on the grass reeds of Clayton's Lake in the early hours of the morning.

OPPOSITE: *Approximately 3 hectares (8 acres) in size, Couran Cove Resort protects the largest remaining patch of Livistona australis rainforest left in south-east Queensland.*
PAGES 74–75: *An elkhorn fern (Platycerium bifurcatum) in the paperbark wetland holds onto its host.*

Fun and Games

Island people have, over the years, had to create their own entertainment. At Roe's Kamp at night, this usually involved a camp fire—around which singing, composing and 'writing romantic poems' passed the hours. Indoor games of cards and 'Up Jenkins', which originated at the Kamp, are still popular today. Early Currigee residents had a hall for dances—with music supplied by accordion, piano or leaf playing. This tradition continues today, with an annual Bush Dance held on the Village Green at Currigee. Outdoor pursuits were freely available—with every form of water sport on hand. A recent migration to the southern end of the island has been the board riders—the Seaway walls having created a favourable break. The Surfrider Foundation is currently awaiting government approval for a Surfing Recreation Reserve in the area.

The Future

Governments at both State and local levels today recognise the recreational value of South Stradbroke Island. All the Crown Land not under lease has become a Conservation Park under the trusteeship of the Gold Coast City Council. Five generations of white settlers and countless generations of Aboriginal people have not destroyed its unique qualities. Sensible planning today will ensure that future generations may enjoy its charm as well.

OPPOSITE: *The outgoing tide provides the most inviting path for early morning joggers as they run towards the daylight.*

At Roe's Kamp (named after a headmaster who established the first permanent holiday spot on the island) students skipping with vines from the dunes, dry off after swimming (1922).
FOLLOWING PAGES: *The aerial roots of the grey mangrove (Avicennia marina) enable this tree to grow in difficult tidal situations.*

Getting Started

Ron Clarke

The graceful tree frog (Litoria gracilenta) can be heard calling from the treetops on warm summer nights.

There were two elements I had not considered before we started to bring the dream into reality—acid sulfate soils and genetic origins of plants for landscaping.

I had never heard of acid sulfate soils, which are prevalent throughout coastal south-east Queensland. When Gold Coast City Councillor David Power, during a very early visit to the site, casually asked me how we were going to treat these soils I could only respond by saying the engineers were preparing a proposal which we would circulate in the next few weeks. I have to admit this remark was made more in hope than knowledge.

When I checked the next day Peter Griffin from Sinclair Knight Merz, the Project Engineers, did say they had a report under way. It recommended we tender the problem out to two reliable operators, requesting detailed submissions on the methods they intended to use.

The conventional option, of physically removing all the suspect sands and soils with its ramifications for the surrounding environment, was not attractive at all. The sheer innovation of Neumann Contractors' submission—

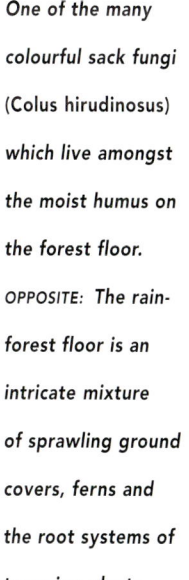

One of the many colourful sack fungi (Colus hirudinosus) which live amongst the moist humus on the forest floor.
OPPOSITE: The rainforest floor is an intricate mixture of sprawling ground covers, ferns and the root systems of towering plants.

The stilted mangrove (Rhizophora stylosa) is responsible for the long, cigar-shaped seed pods found washed up on our coastline.

Never say Never

which recommended separating out the acids, then burying them under water and re-covering them with a metre of sand—interested me, even though (or perhaps because) it was a solution that had never been tried before, anywhere.

Once committed all we had to do was to convince the Gold Coast City Council Officers. I have to say they were open-minded and, while being understandably tough with their monitoring demands, were prepared to accept on face value the evidence presented to them, despite the lack of precedents. I have to pay a great tribute to these usually much-criticised bureaucrats.

It is so easy to have a closed mind and insist that, unless the method has been tried successfully elsewhere, nothing can be approved. We had an unusual problem and, most unbureaucratically, they understood and worked out a way we could at least make a start, without compromising their responsibilities or taking any environmental risks. Initially we submitted twice-daily tests gradually reducing the number as the effectiveness of the method was proven. David Smith, the Site Supervisor from Neumanns, was first-class. He juggled five dredges with ponds seemingly all over the place but which made absolute sense as we worked through to finality.

There was another very important issue I had not thought about sufficiently. During one of our early discussions, the local Chairman of the Australian Conservation Foundation (ACF), Peter Farrell, asked how we intended to plant out the landscaping around all the accommodation areas.

PAGES 84–85: *The march of the soldier crabs (Mictyris sp.) begins at low tide, as they search for food amongst the grains of sand.*

A tiny inhabitant searches the fronds of a fern for its next meal.

OPPOSITE: *The beautiful elkhorn fern (Platycerium bifurcatum) can be found throughout Couran Cove's rainforest and wetland areas.*

Getting Started

As the core of the hotel was to be built on a boardwalk across the top of the weir wall, on 1,500 huge pilings, landscaping was not a factor but it would be essential around the rest of the construction areas—the beaches and the bushland. I had planned to retain a landscaping firm who, when all the construction works were concluded, would landscape whilst all the paths and roads etc. were being built.

The force of the wind alters vegetation in unusual and original ways, such as this flowering paperbark (Melaleuca quinquenervia).

Peter pointed out that as a matter of principle, we should not introduce any exotic plants to South Stradbroke Island. Practically, most plants would find it difficult to survive because of the sand and philosophically, environmentalists believe it is essential that nothing is introduced which could be a threat to the harmony of the present eco-system. Such introduced species also betray the integrity of the setting which had initially attracted us. This all made perfect sense so we agreed to adopt his recommendations.

Then I discovered two other facts of life. Firstly, these indigenous plants were quite expensive if purchased when mature and secondly, genes in plants matter as much as they do in human beings. If we did locate sufficient numbers of the indigenous species we required, at a price that fitted our budget, many may not survive the shock of being introduced to a new habitat. The success rate would be higher if we could grow our own stock by harvesting seeds and taking cuttings from selected plants actually growing on site. The obvious solution was to establish our own nursery.

OPPOSITE: A banksia flower, yet to open, provides a palette of changing colours.

The protected swamp orchid (Phaius tankervilleae) is now becoming common on site.

The vulnerable pink smartweed (Persicaria elatior) is a protected wetland species at Couran Cove.

Our then Site Manager, Tom Caamano, had already started working for us. Tom had been headhunted from his position with the State Department for the Environment after a recommendation to us by Peter Farrell. He was a member of Peter's branch of the ACF on the Gold Coast. Tom set about organising the Nursery and recruiting staff. We were greatly assisted by Glenn Leiper, one of the State's foremost flora specialists and Beth Cooling who, to this day, still assists us in a Consultancy role.

A greenhouse, powered by solar energy with computer-controlled humidity, was immediately established as well as an adjacent protected grow-out area. Very quickly our monthly productivity rate reached 5,000 plants from seeds and cuttings, including success with rare and difficult-to-grow, indigenous plants. One of the successes was the delicate swamp orchid. This was threatened with extinction as the specimens found on South Stradbroke Island, around the rainforest at Couran Cove, are the only remaining ones in Australia.

When we first visited the site we often found holes, some with clearly defined signs of the use of a spade, where these rare orchid specimens should have been growing (proving to us that the thefts were pre-planned and deliberate). We have been able to successfully rehabilitate the orchids so that their population is now into the hundreds rather than the tens. The team has had many other successes and, by the time of opening, there were more than 150,000 various types of attractive indigenous trees, shrubs, flowers and grasses in stock ready to replant around the beaches and Eco-Cabins.

The Nursery staff have also been able to establish a herb garden to assist the kitchen, advance the number of bush tucker plants to enhance the environmental experience, and protect the entire estate by identifying and eradicating the exotic weeds. Staff have also identified a number of plants previously unrecorded on South Stradbroke Island.

The implementation of this simple recommendation from the ACF has been a most useful exercise and the Nursery operation is now an integral part of some of the nature walks which our environmental staff conduct on a thrice-daily basis.

A further feature in this area is the introduction of a 'plant a tree' experience for our younger guests. For a small donation to the Environmental Research Trust Fund they can plant a small sapling of their own choice, from the Nursery stock, which will be duly tagged. In 30 years or so, hopefully they can return and show their children the tree they planted as a tiny tot 'way back in the 20th century'. Even better they can come back each year and plot its progress.

The seed pods of the familiar horsetail oak (Casuarina equisetifolia) have already opened and released their seeds.

The Acid Sulfate Soils

One of the pitfalls about which I was completely unaware, until we started to delve into commencing construction at Couran Cove, was the region's acid sulfate soils. I had no idea what the term meant and was completely horrified when the consultants we had called in told us about the logistics of dredging and treating these soils, which were prolific on the western coast of the site.

The standard treatment involved 240,000 cubic metres of sands which would need to be dredged, piled into trucks and either barged to the mainland or dumped somewhere on the island to be treated with lime in order to sterilise the acid pyrites. If a suitable site could be located the pile would have been about the size of the Melbourne Cricket Ground, and there would need to be 80,000 trips between the treated pile and the harbour. If not, then an equivalent number of barge trips back to the mainland would have been needed. At the going rate of $200 a trip, this meant $16,000,000 just for transport—clearly an impossibility. It looked as though we were defeated before we had even begun.

Then some research led us to Neumann Contractors who had overcome a similar problem whilst constructing a large bridge for the highway across the Tweed River. Although, on that job they didn't actually bury the acid pyrites, as they were proposing to do for us, they were able to substantially reduce the number of truckloads required to transport them off-site by a process of separating sand, water and pyrites.

This was achieved by dredging, then tumbling by pressure hose the dredged material through a series of ponds, where the sands were 'washed' out, culminating in a final settlement pond where the actual pyrites, already separated from the sand content in the water, settled to the bottom after a few hours. Reduced quantities though they were, we still needed to find a way to store and treat this acidic end product. A simple solution was presented—one that had never been tried before, anywhere in the world.

Why not bury them (the pyrites) back under the water (where they are harmless as they only become poisonous when exposed to oxygen)? We could then cover them with a metre of clean sand so they would never present a danger. What's more we could use the same sands that had been separated out whilst isolating the acids.

So that's what we did. As a world first we were able to ensure the entire construction area was free of acid sulfates by separating, then burying them under a layer of sand and water.

Neumanns presented their proven concept, once they had completed our project, to their industry's international journal. Australian industry was able to chalk up another world-first innovation.

And we were able to get on with building the Resort of our dreams.

Treatment of Acid Sulfate Soils

When exposed to oxygen through earthworks or building, affected soil can produce an acidic content which pollutes or poisons waterways and wetlands. To overcome this an innovative treatment of acid sulfate soils was pioneered at Couran Cove.

STAGE 1 (right)
- The dredging operation removes all solid material from the harbour.
- Sand and silts contain the pyrites which generate acid once exposed to the air.

STAGE 3 (below right)
- Disposal pit is excavated out beneath the harbour wall.
- The pit is then used for final disposition of silts.
- Silts permanently stored in pit beneath a sand capping and in an anaerobic environment.
- Silts are pumped into pit using tailwater pump (shown in STAGE 2) and discharged below the water surface with no visible turbulence.
- Clean, white, freshly washed sand now covers the entire base of the Resort's harbour and lagoon. The land and sea around remain undisturbed.

STAGE 2 (below)
- Sand and silt slurry is pumped to the reclamation site.
- During dredging and filling, the silts are separated from the sand grains.
- 'Dirty' water is drained off to the temporary storage ponds for later disposal.
- Reclamation is set up so there are no ponding areas and the sands are washed away freely.

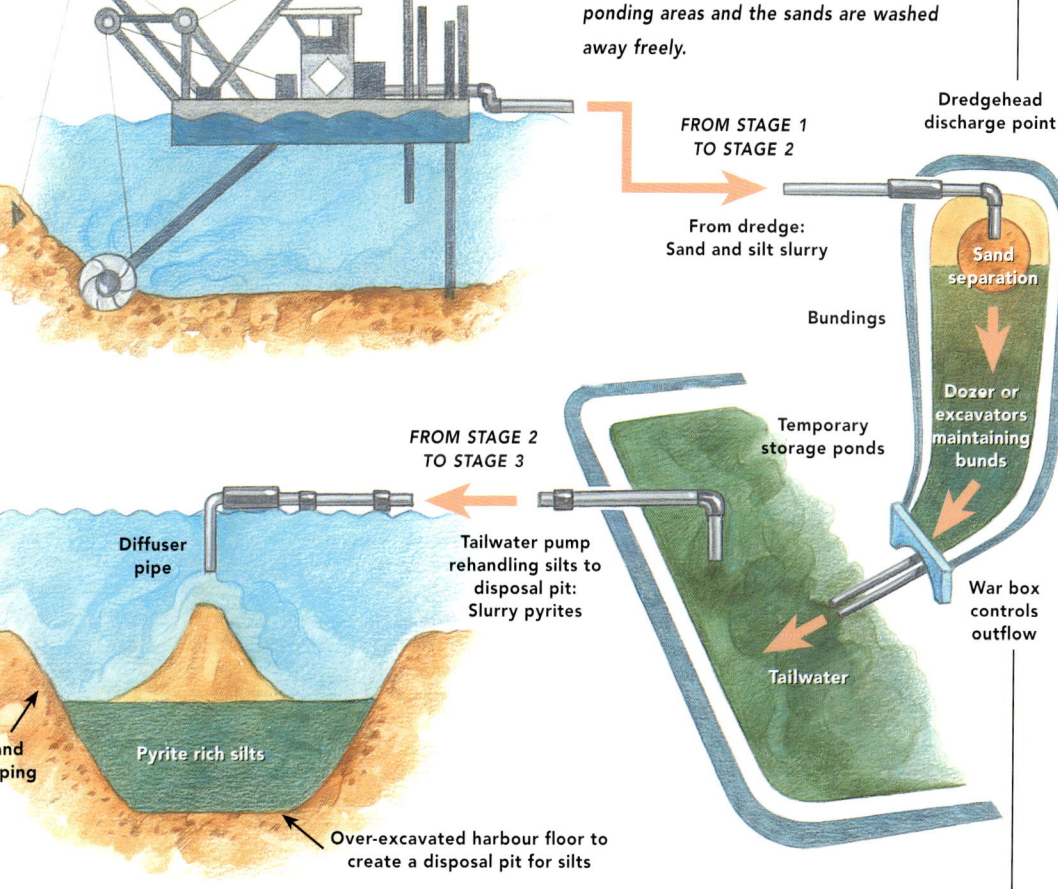

PREVIOUS PAGES:
The first facility built, the Native Plant Nursery has provided plants for landscaping after construction and for revegetating areas damaged by past farming practices.

The common crow (Euploea core) is one of the many resident butterflies seen at the Resort.

The Nursery

The Resort uses only native plant species endemic to South Stradbroke Island. The Nursery, which began in August 1996, propagates over 5,000 species per month. All the seeds, spores and cuttings—from rare, threatened and once-common plants—used for propagation, come from the Couran Cove site thus ensuring integrity of genetic lines. The plants are then used to landscape the Resort and rehabilitate sites altered or damaged by fire, theft and farming.

Plantings from the Nursery have a higher success rate of surviving, use less water, require minimal or no fertilisers and will reduce the need for long-term maintenance. The landscapes provide corridors for the wildlife.

Identifying and eradicating weed species are important aspects of rehabilitation. Chemicals are not used. Weeds are manually extracted (highly labour intensive) then replaced with plants from the Nursery and mulched with organic matter.

Natural remedies, not chemicals, are used in the Nursery itself. A specific biological method of pest control is the propagation of an anti-mosquito/sandfly plant called the sandfly bush (our main method of mosquito management is discussed later in the book). We are also eradicating introduced bees and replacing them with native bees which don't sting (to pollinate certain plant species); rehabilitating native butterfly numbers by the use of host species planting (such as the native violet); and promoting the viability of native frogs by building a cane toad-proof fence around Frog Lake.

Couran Cove Revegetation Cycle

CLOCKWISE FROM TOP

1. Seeds and cuttings collected.
2. Seeds and cuttings placed in propagation dome.
3. Seeds germinate and cuttings take root in propagation dome.
4. Seedlings and cuttings in tubers placed in shadehouse.
5. Potted plants placed in grow-out area.
6. Plants used to landscape.

PREVIOUS PAGES: *The wallabies make their presence felt, from the western coast and mangroves, to the eastern beach and foredunes.*

Rehabilitation and Weed Control

Many vegetation areas within the Couran Cove Resort area are being rehabilitated with plants from the Nursery.

Mangrove swamps and salt marshes protect and stabilise our coastal areas, as well as provide a habitat for many fish species and a source of food for many native animals and birds. Previously much of the area was cleared and is now being restored.

Paperbark (Melaleuca) swamps, found in lowland coastal areas, were often regarded by the old settlers as unattractive, mosquito breeding grounds. They provide a buffer zone between our shoreline, estuaries and river systems. Their removal in the past caused increased runoff and nutrient concentrations, deterioration of aquatic eco-systems, loss of wildlife habitat and possible exposure of acid sulfate soils. Their understorey has a variety of ferns, grasses, orchids and epiphytes. The extensive root system of the paperbarks creates sediment mounds which allows the germination and survival of less water-tolerant plants, such as the cabbage-tree palm (*Livistona australis*).

Pacific Ocean

N

- Livistona rainforest
- Melaleuca/Livistona forest
- Disturbed areas
- Eucalyptus/Melaleuca forest
- Mixed eucalypt woodland
- Melaleuca quinquenervia forest
- Casuarina equisetifolia forest
- Banksia/Casuarina forest
- Spinifex grassland
- Mangroves
- Sedgeland

The Broadwater

LEFT: **Vegetation types on the Couran Cove site.** *(plotted by the Australian Conservation Foundation)*

Getting Started

Eucalypt woodlands on South Stradbroke Island with some rainforest trees have created a unique environment in which the Eco-Cabins are situated. There was minimal impact on the environment during construction—all mature trees were left—and there is continued protection of the habitat by use of tracks around trees—to decrease erosion and plant damage.

Coastal dunes must be carefully managed with an emphasis on minimal construction. Sandmining of the coastal dunes altered the shape of the natural dune system and resulted in large depressions every 100 metres. The large pond, Clayton's Lake, behind the hind dune on the eastern beach is a reminder of this activity. After mining, a rehabilitation program was initiated but was mostly unsuccessful because the mobile dunes kept engulfing the plants, the remaining wild cattle grazed on the vegetation and some species, not endemic to the island, were inappropriate. Couran Cove Resort is currently rehabilitating the dune system with spinifex and sedge from the Nursery which will assist in the overall stabilisation.

Over the past 200 years many plant species have been depleted because of cattle grazing, agriculture, fire and timber cutting. Couran Cove Resort is helping to restore the balance by implementing extensive rehabilitation programs and protective measures for all vegetation types found within the site. The results will enable us all to enjoy this beautiful place now and in the future.

The twisted shapes of many gum trees show individual character.

BELOW & FOLLOWING PAGES: *The photograph below is a miniature of the following six pages, which shows an undistorted panoramic 360° view of the* Livistona australis *rainforest. Experience the rainforest as if you are there and are turning a full circle.*

Protecting the Environment

The Challenges

Ron Clarke

The handsome saw-leaf banksia (Banksia serrata) is common throughout the woodland areas of the Resort.

'You can never retain environmental purity and develop a large resort' is probably the most ridiculous statement we encountered on our path of taking Couran Cove from dream to reality.

What is a large resort?

If a small resort can be ecologically pure, then what if you put two or three or even six 'ecologically pure' resorts side by side. Do they lose their status because they are next to another similar resort? If so, why? If not, then could not a large resort be merely an amalgamation of a number of smaller ones? Many 'Greenies', who alleged that about Couran Cove Resort, had one thing in common—they never visited us to see for themselves. None ever specified just why size mattered.

Being an Accountant, I am trained to consider that size can

The nocturnal brown tree snake (Boiga irregularis) is harmless to humans.
OPPOSITE: This shield bug nymph (Family Pentatomidae) is usually found on the trunks of eucalypts.

A rainforest dominated by cabbage-tree palms (Livistona australis) is the most significant patch of vegetation at the Couran Cove site.

be an asset rather than a liability because of the economies that can be effected.

Our very size allowed us to purchase a rubbish compactor unit, to sort out and compact non-organic matter into easily disposable packages, and to transport it back to the mainland. It allowed us to introduce a vermiculture unit (utilising over a million worms to convert organic waste into usable fertiliser)—small resorts cannot justify the expenditure. Especially it permitted us to introduce an Energy Management Control System, the first of its kind worldwide, and develop revolutionary pest control methodologies that should become mandatory throughout south-eastern Queensland.

A journalist, in a recent newspaper article, after viewing a lifestyle television program which featured our Resort, expounded her theory—a common one amongst environmentalists—that Couran Cove could not be an Eco-Tourist Resort. Not only because it was too large but also because it was too comfortable and had too many facilities.

The view was that 'eco-tourism' can only be experienced by visiting the 'real bush' and camping on the ground, swatting flies, having no toilet or hot water, with only the camp fire to cook on, and nothing else to do but observe nature. It wasn't mentioned, but eco-tourists usually don't travel anywhere without the aid of their four-wheel-drive vehicles, which knock down shrubs and frighten away the wildlife they have come to observe.

PAGES 110–111: *Basking in the sun is a popular pastime for lace monitors* (Varanus varius) *which can grow to one-and-a-half metres.*

The sacred kingfisher (Todiramphus sancta) **perches on a vantage point overlooking the western foreshore.**

OPPOSITE: The agile wallaby (Macropus agilis) *grazes on most forms of native vegetation, even the leaves of mangroves.*

Getting Started

As the core of the hotel was to be built on a boardwalk across the top of the weir wall, on 1,500 huge pilings, landscaping was not a factor but it would be essential around the rest of the construction areas—the beaches and the bushland. I had planned to retain a landscaping firm who, when all the construction works were concluded, would landscape whilst all the paths and roads etc. were being built.

Peter pointed out that as a matter of principle, we should not introduce any exotic plants to South Stradbroke Island. Practically, most plants would find it difficult to survive because of the sand and philosophically, environmentalists believe it is essential that nothing is introduced which could be a threat to the harmony of the present eco-system. Such introduced species also betray the integrity of the setting which had initially attracted us. This all made perfect sense so we agreed to adopt his recommendations.

The force of the wind alters vegetation in unusual and original ways, such as this flowering paperbark (Melaleuca quinquenervia).

Then I discovered two other facts of life. Firstly, these indigenous plants were quite expensive if purchased when mature and secondly, genes in plants matter as much as they do in human beings. If we did locate sufficient numbers of the indigenous species we required, at a price that fitted our budget, many may not survive the shock of being introduced to a new habitat. The success rate would be higher if we could grow our own stock by harvesting seeds and taking cuttings from selected plants actually growing on site. The obvious solution was to establish our own nursery.

OPPOSITE: *A banksia flower, yet to open, provides a palette of changing colours.*

Protecting the Environment

So let me set down my ideas about eco-tourism and environmentally based resorts:

1. I detest what four-wheel-drive vehicles do to the bush and see no need for them. If you want to get away from civilisation so desperately, then walk and carry in your requirements—a sleeping bag, a small tent, some food and a canteen of water. But four-wheelers and the environment are, to my mind, mutually exclusive. There are none at Couran Cove Resort.

2. I do not see the need to sleep in discomfort. Tents may be okay with proper beds, but what has lying in an awkward, uncomfortable position, without proper toilet or cooking facilities, to do with the environment? Surely these are matters of personal choice and hygiene? It is the setting in which you camp which is the attraction, not the camping. At Couran Cove we have all types of accommodation but they have a common theme—access to good food, spotlessly clean facilities, plenty of varying activities, and complete comfort, and sites the casual camper could travel hundreds of kilometres to find and never duplicate.

3. Another claim in the newspaper article seemed to be that without being bitten by mosquitoes and sandflies, or being driven silly by small bush flies, or risking your life by trampling through the bush ignoring the possibility of being bitten by poisonous snakes, you were somehow missing out on experiencing the true Australian bush.

The royal spoonbill (Platalea regia) wades through the wetland areas of Couran Cove, and roosts in adjacent trees.

OPPOSITE:
On the edge of the mangroves.

The Acid Sulfate Soils

One of the pitfalls about which I was completely unaware, until we started to delve into commencing construction at Couran Cove, was the region's acid sulfate soils. I had no idea what the term meant and was completely horrified when the consultants we had called in told us about the logistics of dredging and treating these soils, which were prolific on the western coast of the site.

The standard treatment involved 240,000 cubic metres of sands which would need to be dredged, piled into trucks and either barged to the mainland or dumped somewhere on the island to be treated with lime in order to sterilise the acid pyrites. If a suitable site could be located the pile would have been about the size of the Melbourne Cricket Ground, and there would need to be 80,000 trips between the treated pile and the harbour. If not, then an equivalent number of barge trips back to the mainland would have been needed. At the going rate of $200 a trip, this meant $16,000,000 just for transport—clearly an impossibility. It looked as though we were defeated before we had even begun.

Then some research led us to Neumann Contractors who had overcome a similar problem whilst constructing a large bridge for the highway across the Tweed River. Although, on that job they didn't actually bury the acid pyrites, as they were proposing to do for us, they were able to substantially reduce the number of truckloads required to transport them off-site by a process of separating sand, water and pyrites.

This was achieved by dredging, then tumbling by pressure hose the dredged material through a series of ponds, where the sands were 'washed' out, culminating in a final settlement pond where the actual pyrites, already separated from the sand content in the water, settled to the bottom after a few hours. Reduced quantities though they were, we still needed to find a way to store and treat this acidic end product. A simple solution was presented—one that had never been tried before, anywhere in the world.

Why not bury them (the pyrites) back under the water (where they are harmless as they only become poisonous when exposed to oxygen)? We could then cover them with a metre of clean sand so they would never present a danger. What's more we could use the same sands that had been separated out whilst isolating the acids.

So that's what we did. As a world first we were able to ensure the entire construction area was free of acid sulfates by separating, then burying them under a layer of sand and water.

Neumanns presented their proven concept, once they had completed our project, to their industry's international journal. Australian industry was able to chalk up another world-first innovation.

And we were able to get on with building the Resort of our dreams.

Treatment of Acid Sulfate Soils

When exposed to oxygen through earthworks or building, affected soil can produce an acidic content which pollutes or poisons waterways and wetlands. To overcome this an innovative treatment of acid sulfate soils was pioneered at Couran Cove.

STAGE 1 (right)
- The dredging operation removes all solid material from the harbour.
- Sand and silts contain the pyrites which generate acid once exposed to the air.

STAGE 3 (below right)
- Disposal pit is excavated out beneath the harbour wall.
- The pit is then used for final disposition of silts.
- Silts permanently stored in pit beneath a sand capping and in an anaerobic environment.
- Silts are pumped into pit using tailwater pump (shown in STAGE 2) and discharged below the water surface with no visible turbulence.
- Clean, white, freshly washed sand now covers the entire base of the Resort's harbour and lagoon. The land and sea around remain undisturbed.

STAGE 2 (below)
- Sand and silt slurry is pumped to the reclamation site.
- During dredging and filling, the silts are separated from the sand grains.
- 'Dirty' water is drained off to the temporary storage ponds for later disposal.
- Reclamation is set up so there are no ponding areas and the sands are washed away freely.

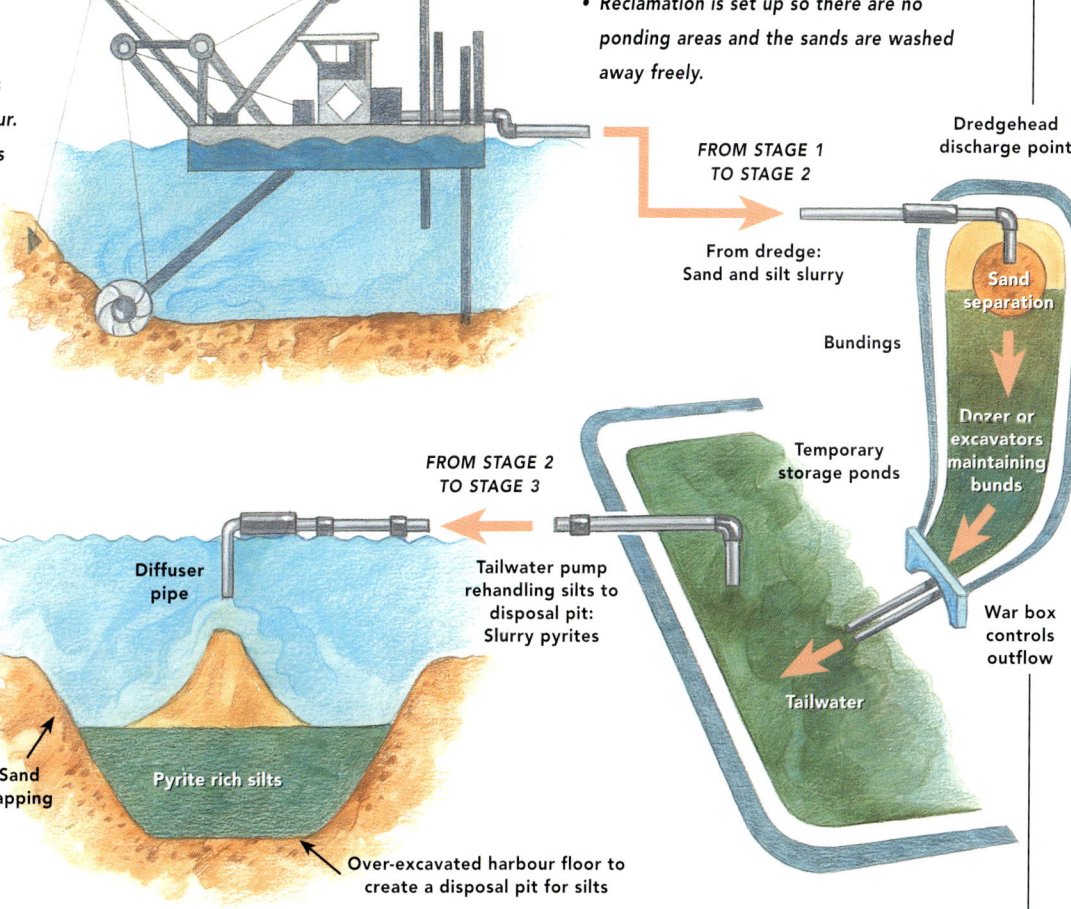

PREVIOUS PAGES: *The first facility built, the Native Plant Nursery has provided plants for landscaping after construction and for revegetating areas damaged by past farming practices.*

The common crow (Euploea core) is one of the many resident butterflies seen at the Resort.

The Nursery

The Resort uses only native plant species endemic to South Stradbroke Island. The Nursery, which began in August 1996, propagates over 5,000 species per month. All the seeds, spores and cuttings—from rare, threatened and once-common plants—used for propagation, come from the Couran Cove site thus ensuring integrity of genetic lines. The plants are then used to landscape the Resort and rehabilitate sites altered or damaged by fire, theft and farming.

Plantings from the Nursery have a higher success rate of surviving, use less water, require minimal or no fertilisers and will reduce the need for long-term maintenance. The landscapes provide corridors for the wildlife.

Identifying and eradicating weed species are important aspects of rehabilitation. Chemicals are not used. Weeds are manually extracted (highly labour intensive) then replaced with plants from the Nursery and mulched with organic matter.

Natural remedies, not chemicals, are used in the Nursery itself. A specific biological method of pest control is the propagation of an anti-mosquito/sandfly plant called the sandfly bush (our main method of mosquito management is discussed later in the book). We are also eradicating introduced bees and replacing them with native bees which don't sting (to pollinate certain plant species); rehabilitating native butterfly numbers by the use of host species planting (such as the native violet); and promoting the viability of native frogs by building a cane toad-proof fence around Frog Lake.

Getting Started

Couran Cove Revegetation Cycle

CLOCKWISE FROM TOP

1. Seeds and cuttings collected.
2. Seeds and cuttings placed in propagation dome.
3. Seeds germinate and cuttings take root in propagation dome.
4. Seedlings and cuttings in tubers placed in shadehouse.
5. Potted plants placed in grow-out area.
6. Plants used to landscape.

The water management

Water supply

South Stradbroke Island, like its neighbour North Stradbroke and cousin Fraser Island, are entirely sand. Consequently they are all huge water reservoirs. The sand has accumulated over millions of years on a rock base some 30 to 50 metres below ground level and the island's rainfall filters down through the layers of sand to the rock face and then out to the nearest waterway.

At our Resort, on the eastern ocean side, the watertable is so close to the surface that natural freshwater perpetual lakes form wherever a deep indentation in the land surface has occurred. There is one (Clayton's Lake) just 50 metres or so from the surf between the primary and secondary sand dunes, adjacent to the Oceanman Surf Club.

It is estimated South Stradbroke has sufficient water stores at any one time to support 5,000 residents for 12 months without further rainfall. North Stradbroke exports around 100,000 litres a year to neighbouring islands. This does not mean we should squander any of what is, after all, mankind's most precious and indispensable asset. One of the major reasons for discarding the developmental approval we had for the building of a golf course at the Resort, was the amount of water such a facility would require.

The treatment methods we use ensure the water mined is sufficiently 'pure' for our guests. I suspect the natural state of the water, including all the so-called pollutants, is better for us to drink than the purified version our government authorities insist we reticulate.

Clayton's Lake, showing the delicate fresh water of South Stradbroke Island, was formed as a result of past sandmining.

Water treatment

Water is extracted from an underlying aquifer and pumped to a raw water storage tank. Water is treated by a Nanofiltration Plant. This reverse osmosis process produces ultra-pure drinking water of a standard similar to bottled drinking water. Nanofiltration ensures minimal chlorine is required for disinfection as it removes 99% of organic compounds which react with chlorine. Three days of water supply is stored in clean water tanks which is then pumped throughout the Resort. All reject water is used to irrigate gardens and landscaped areas. Nanofiltration uses minimal chemical input and minimal energy demand.

ABOVE: *Reject water is used for new native plantings in revegetated areas.*
BELOW: *Two 700,000-litre water-holding tanks ensure the Resort has a steady flow of treated water.*

BELOW: *This Water Purification Treatment Plant produces water for the Resort.*

The energy management

The most important element of our ecological initiatives was the minimising of the power usage and the reduction of Greenhouse Gas Emissions. We searched high and low for engineering consultants who shared our philosophies and who had the expertise and proven experience to implement their ideas.

Firstly a decision was made to use LPG (liquefied petroleum gas) rather than diesel fuel to ensure the inevitable spillages or leaks would not affect any of the Resort's environment; an early inquiry to SEQEB (the local power authority) as to the feasibility of an underwater cable connection to the mainland electricity grid revealed it was economically impossible—we were quoted a figure in excess of $12 million. This was twice the cost of building our own generator powerhouse and infrastructure.

Then we had Frank Barram and his team at Integrated Energy Systems (IES) examine every light, every piece of equipment and each item requiring power to ensure they used the lowest possible energy output without compromising any efficiency of purpose.

But the real master stroke was the introduction of another engineering consultancy to us by IES. Measurement Engineering

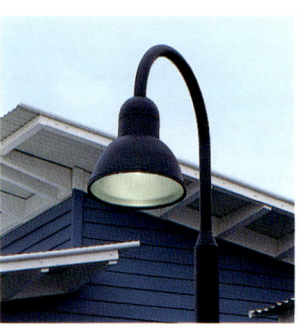

specialise in innovative energy systems. They designed the pacing lights and automatic timing devices/display boards on our 180-metre Resort Running Sprint Track.

IES's brief was to establish a software computer system that would monitor the five generators and the individual demand generated by each and all accommodation and community service areas so that, if necessary in periods of high loads, some items can be turned off sequentially for short periods to avoid an excess demand.

An added bonus to this constant monitoring is the ability we have to keep each unit of accommodation—be it a Marine Apartment, a Lodge or Villa, or even an Eco-Cabin—aware of how much power it has used during every 24-hour period (the graph, available on the guests' television screen, is

ABOVE: *Every electrical item in the Resort has been checked for power consumption and efficiency, even the street lights.*
LEFT: *The 180-metre Sprint Track has pacing lights and photo-electric timing.*

Protecting the Environment

updated by the computer every 10 minutes). This allows us to look to educating our guests as to the number of kilowatt hours they are consuming. To add extra interest we are setting a target standard depending upon the type of accommodation, and the number of adults occupying it. If the target is exceeded, their bill will be increased by $1 for each kilowatt hour in excess. These monies will be deposited into our Environmental Research Trust Fund (which we established in May 1998 with a $50,000 donation).

The accommodation units which use the least per adult per 24 hours in each calendar month will be rewarded with a complimentary holiday for the same length of time and for the same number of adults.

For the Resort, we have saved on the generator capacity we would otherwise have been statutorily required to provide (a saving in excess of $1 million); the greenhouse gases have been lowered by an estimated 7,000,000 kg annually; and our operational and maintenance costs will be reduced by more than $500,000 over normal costs.

And they say being environmental costs more. We have proven that there are savings to be made.

LEFT: *The on-screen display illustrates power consumption.*
RIGHT: *Gas heating is a feature in the Eco-Cabins.*
BELOW: *Energy efficient lighting is used throughout the Resort.*

Energy savings

- Up-front capital costs were reduced by $2.5 million and operating costs of $1 million are saved annually.
- Power demand is one-third of similar-sized resorts.
- Primary energy use is down by 60% and greenhouse gas emissions have been reduced by over 70%.
- A household at the Resort uses 25% of the energy of a normal Queensland household.
- All appliances and lighting are selected according to their energy efficiency to maximise power savings.
- Hot water comes from gas-boosted solar water heaters.
- Passive solar design is used in all buildings, including natural lighting and careful building orientation.
- Ceiling and wall insulation and shading minimise heat gain.
- Super-energy efficient lights and lighting control systems are used and public areas are only lit when occupied.
- Gas is used for cooking.
- Rooms are heated by gas appliances.
- Water-efficient devices save water.
- Super-efficient motors drive airconditioning and refrigeration.
- The main kitchen has a gas dishwasher.

ABOVE & BELOW: All Eco-Cabins have solar hot-water systems which reduce water heating costs by up to 80%.

Five small 150 kVA gas generators provide power at 10% of the emissions of diesel ones.

Five control boxes, in front of the generators, monitor their performance.

Gas is not only used for cooking but also powers the dishwasher in the main kitchen.

Protecting the Environment

Advanced Energy System

This is a cost-effective, yet sustainable, energy system. The Resort generates its own power from a combination of wind (12%), gas (48.8%) and other renewable and low impact technologies, including solar power and using waste heat (39.2%).

LPG storage tanks power the generators, fire all gas appliances in the kitchens, accommodation units and other facilities.

The largest commercial wind turbine in Queensland supplements power to the generators at the Main Station.

Generators at the Main Station supply power to all facilities and appliances carefully selected for power-saving qualities.

The centralised Energy Management Control System is a computer program that monitors power usage and optimises energy use by switching on and off generators. It spreads loads during peak periods by switching off non-essential appliances for short periods. Waste heat from generators is used for heating pools in winter months.

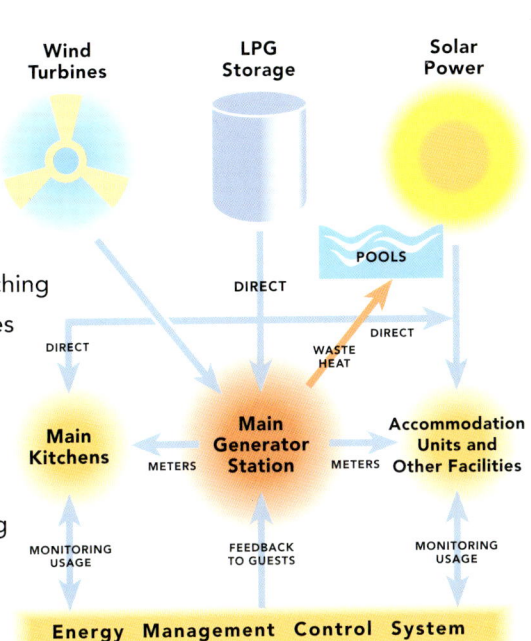

LEFT: Analysis of wind data demonstrated that wind was a viable alternative and would save 137 tonnes of LPG per annum.

BELOW: The LPG storage tank. Using LPG saves greenhouse gas emissions, fossil fuel use and reduces noise pollution.

The waste management

An island adds an extra dimension to civilisation's continuing challenge to control its own waste products. Traditionally sewage is pumped into rivers and disgorged into the ocean untreated. Household rubbish is discarded into bins, collected by councils, piled up in a local tip, then buried.

There was no way we wanted to be involved in these sorts of options. So we looked for a more suitable sewage treatment system that, for a wide variety of daily usage volumes, could cope and treat to a tertiary, potable product level.

Our people found a system that had been developed by a company in New South Wales and had installed them in a number of NSW townships. It is called Enviroflow. This system has the advantage of operating efficiently with a relatively small throughput. (Normally in sewage treatment plants the higher and more consistent the input, the more efficiently the treatment process works.)

To be certain all the nasties had been eliminated we added a UV treatment unit and an irrigation system which circulated the output over a wide area of bushland through an underground pipe system with a drip-feed output.

Every facility at the Resort is required to carefully separate their waste, even the lifeguards on the surf beach.

The second arm of waste management is the disposal of food scraps, packaging, etc. An efficient collection system is required, with secure public bins so birds and animals cannot be attracted to them. Then a large depot is needed, centrally sited for ease of collection, where rubbish can be sorted and compacted to minimise the volume transported back to the mainland.

We became very interested in Vermiculture. It seemed to make sense to harness nature itself in order to dispose of waste food and other organic refuse. For the rest, a compacting plant is the perfect way to reduce the size of the problem to make it manageable.

At the Resort these back-of-house facilities are not hidden away from prying eyes—rather we invite guests, if they are so inclined, to see the efficiency, cleanliness and the innovations incorporated into the methods we have selected to dispose of their rubbish.

Protecting the Environment

Waste Management

Waste Minimisation
- Purchasing policy
- Workplace practices

↓

Waste Segregation at Source
- Minimise double handling
- Education of staff & guests

↓

Waste Collection
Regular bin collection & cleaning to maintain aesthetics & reduce odours

↓

Waste Storage & Transport
Segregated wastes stockpiled & sent to recyclers

Non-Recyclable
- Waste compacted to minimise barge space & costs
- Organic waste, cold stored & batch quantities weighed

→ **Dumping Cost Minimisation**
- To recyclers—cardboard, paper, cans & bottles (plastic & glass)
- To landfill—compacted waste

→ **Organic Waste**
- Screened & puréed to reduce particle size
- Mixed with lime seolite, green waste & cardboard for aeration & odour reduction

↓

Composting Process
- 3000-litre tumbler with forced air induction
- Heat kills seeds & pathogens
- Begins breakdown process

↓

Vermiculture System
- Material fed to worm beds turned to worm castings
- Finished product—worms & worm castings—harvested

→ **Product Use**
Soil conditioner for nursery, landscape & food systems

Product Sales
Surplus sold—worms & castings

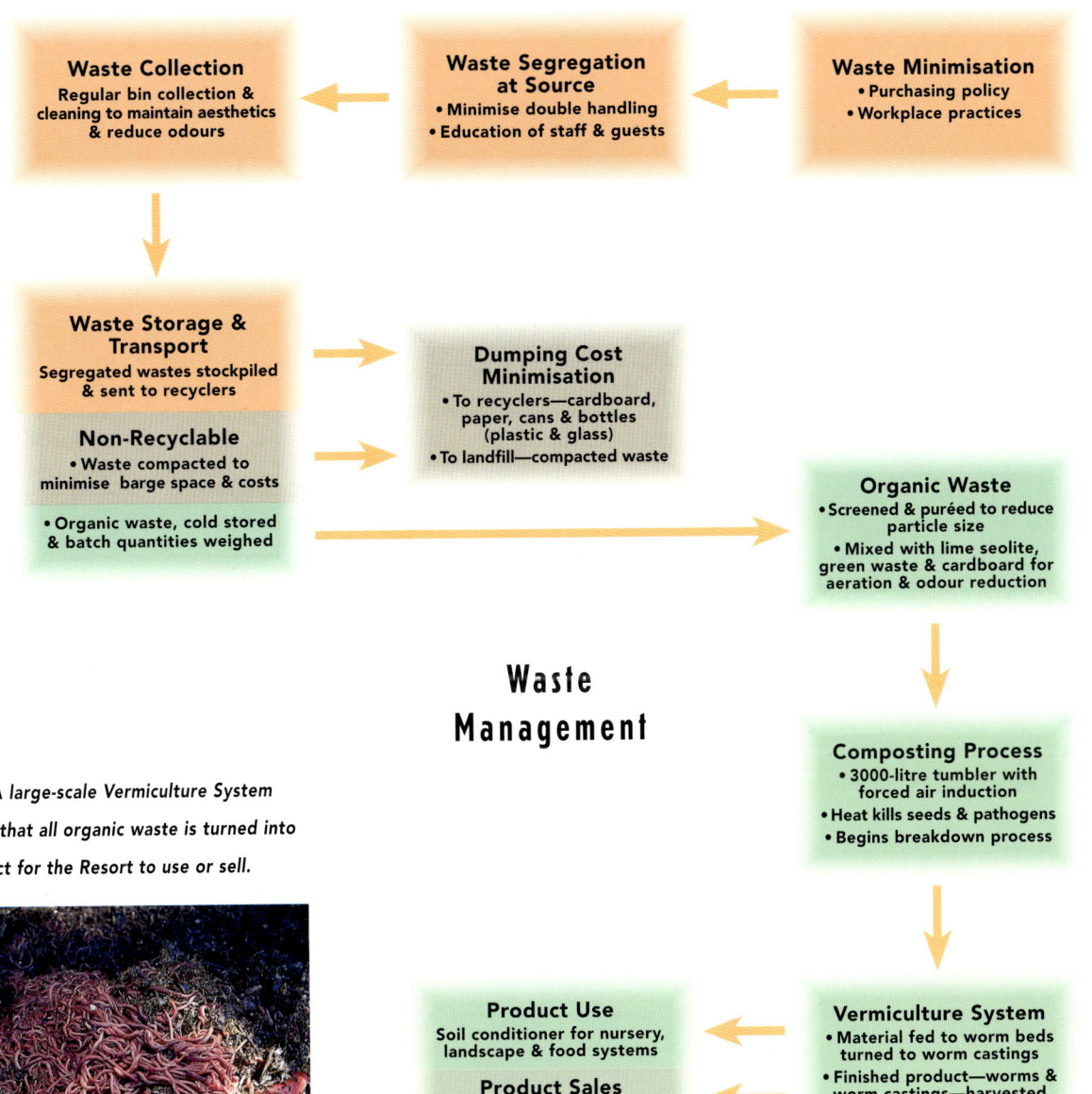

BELOW: A large-scale Vermiculture System ensures that all organic waste is turned into a product for the Resort to use or sell.

General waste

All waste collected is sorted into recyclables, solid waste or organic waste. Recyclables from the kitchens and accommodation areas are collected and stored for transportation back to the mainland. Solid waste from the kitchens and accommodation areas are compacted and returned to the mainland. Organic waste from the kitchen is pulped then liquid from the pulping goes to the sewage treatment plant and solids go to the worm farm. Garden waste is shredded, composted and put into the worm farm.

WASTE MANAGEMENT HIERARCHY

AVOIDING excess waste and decreasing waste disposal volumes is the key component of the Waste Management Program. Couran Cove Resort purchases in bulk and the General Store sells in bulk packaging, if possible, rather than using pre-printed or manufactured packages.

RE-USE extends the life of a product and decreases waste in the landfill. Organic waste is put through the Vermiculture System (worm farm) then used as fertiliser and soil conditioner.

RECYCLE and hopefully decrease the amount of virgin materials required. All recyclables are collected, sorted, compacted and shipped to the mainland for recycling.

DISPOSAL of waste is the least desirable aspect. Some waste goes to landfill, but at Couran Cove Resort there is continual seeking of alternatives and program implementation to decrease this component.

Sewage

At the Resort collection, treatment and disposal of sewage waste goes far beyond industry and government standards.

COLLECTION

The Vacuum Sewer System, with minimal vegetation and soil disturbance, involves sewage being gravity fed from housing to central collection areas using shallow trenches. The ability of the Vacuum Sewer System to lift sewage up hills reduces the trenching depth and minimises negative environmental impacts that would arise with conventional collection systems with their deeper and wider trenches.

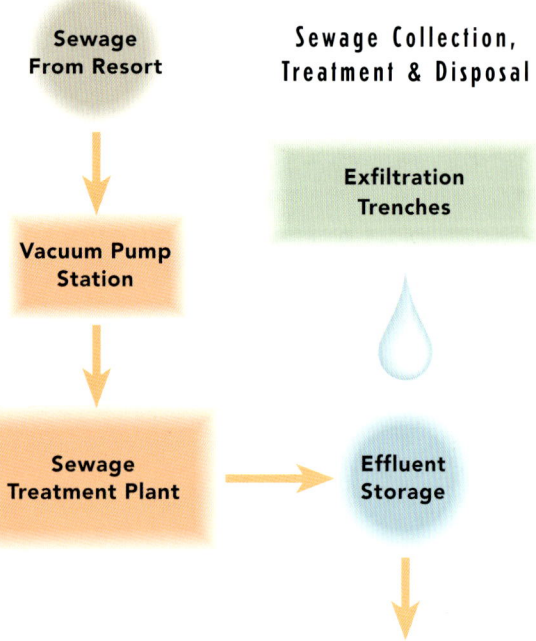

Sewage Collection, Treatment & Disposal

Protecting the Environment

TREATMENT

The treatment plant consists of 4 major components: primary, secondary, tertiary and then a final polishing process. The polishing process results in water that is fit for human consumption (potable). The Resort's treatment system is based on a combination of the Enviroflow down-flow trickling biofilter and the Dynasand up-flow activated sand filter as well as UV disinfection.

- Enviroflow biofilter, or down-flow trickling filter, is a standard and effective secondary treatment. Achieves secondary standard effluent including the process of nitrification (converting ammonia into nitrate).
- Dynasand denitrifying tertiary filter, which converts nitrate into nitrogen gas (denitrification), is an up-flow sand filter which is continuously monitored and fed a carbon source.

The Enviroflow tanks and associated systems convert the Resort's sewage into potable irrigation water.

- UV disinfection gives a 99.99% kill rate. This effective disinfection process was selected because minimal input is required, there are no side effects or no vegetation clearing requirements.

EFFLUENT & SLUDGE DISPOSAL

Treated effluent is stored and re-used through drip irrigation (using underground drippers) to maintain the Resort's vegetation, the Sports Oval and the green fire break needed for management of potential fire hazards.

Sludge produced is processed and introduced into the Vermiculture System (worm farm) for conversion into compost.

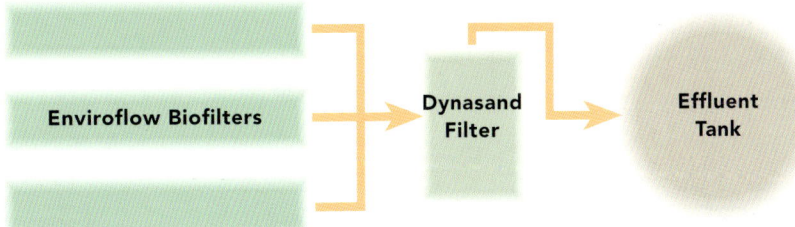

Stages of Sewage Treatment

Overcoming the pests: mosquitoes

The good news is there are virtually no flies on the island, although South Straddie is renowned for its mosquito population. The proximity of the Broadwater, with its mangrove swamps, and the scattered freshwater lakes in and about the rainforest enclaves, guaranteed an over abundance of these pests.

But fog spraying, often the only response of mainland councils, was not an option—it doesn't last and affects other small harmless insects that are so important to the natural environment.

At the same time we were not about to spend $150 million building a Resort to which no one would come because of its mosquitoes.

The solution is a large-scale, environmentally friendly approach to pest management. This outstandingly effective approach is three-pronged:

- We deny the larvae and mature mosquitoes feeding opportunities.
- We treat their breeding areas to sterilise their larvae thus preventing reproduction.
- We encourage natural predators such as mini-bats and Pacific blue-eye fish, both of whom regard mosquitoes and mosquito larvae as a special treat and, if it is available, devote all their active hours seeking it out and devouring it.

The 76 light traps, specially built to catch mosquitoes, are an innovation unique to Couran Cove. Our pest management consultants collect the nets each morning, identify the type of pest and thus the probable location of its breeding ground (via our computer program), go and treat this area with a special bio-organic natural substance which sterilises the larvae or with Pacific blue-eye fish

Wetland areas on site, such as this pond near the western foreshore, are carefully monitored for mosquito breeding.

which eat the larvae, thus eliminating the problem.

So successful has this program been that the only problem now is mosquitoes being blown in from neighbouring sites. Consequently, we are expanding our treatment areas to incorporate adjacent properties, especially those upwind.

Mosquito management

Mosquito management involves:
- monitoring the watertable and pooling areas, where the mosquitoes breed
- monitoring wind direction, as mosquitoes can be blown on site
- careful development of the Resort's buildings and facilities, with special consideration to harbour sites where mosquitoes might live
- use of natural predators, such as the Pacific blue-eye fish which eat mosquito larvae
- development and use of the Mosquito Light Trap

The Living Resources Mosquito Light Trap

This major innovation, developed by our Pest Management Consultant, Dave Piggott, is a great success. It is solar powered, battery operated, utilises carbon dioxide with an ultraviolet light, a suction fan and a net. This is an alternative to the traditional 'zapper' which is not species specific and makes species identification difficult.

HOW IT WORKS

Most mosquitoes are attracted to carbon dioxide (which is why they are attracted to humans). The solar-powered light traps are baited with dry ice (carbon dioxide) thus attracting the mosquitoes, they move to the ultraviolet light, the fan sucks them into the net. Daily identification leads to subsequent eradication in the breeding grounds.

Mosquito Life Cycle

There are 10 identified species on South Stradbroke Island, found in containers, groundwater and ponds, polluted (grey) water, drains and salt marsh. The oviposition site must contain water for the aquatic (larval) stages and have no predators, otherwise the female will seek a more suitable site, if available.

EGG STAGE
Females lay up to 300 eggs.

LARVAL STAGE
Larvae goes through 4 size changes, each change is dependent on water temperature. Hormonal larvicide is applied at this stage.

PUPAL STAGE
Final change to adult, takes a minimum of 1 day.

ADULT STAGE
Female seeks a host from which to extract blood to incubate eggs and male feeds only on flower nectar.

Bringing it all Together

Introduction

Ron Clarke

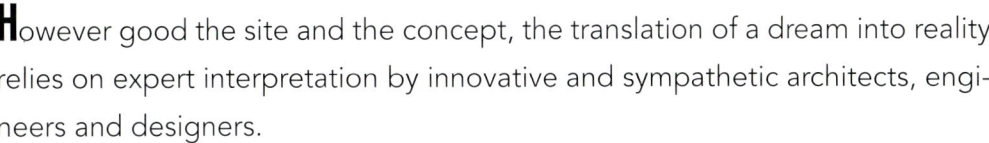

Each apartment has its own extensive balcony well screened from its neighbours.

However good the site and the concept, the translation of a dream into reality relies on expert interpretation by innovative and sympathetic architects, engineers and designers.

The team we assembled, led by Daryl Jackson, was first-class. I mentioned earlier in the book how Daryl's and my friendship dates back to Essendon State School when, as nine year olds, we were not only classmates but shared the same desk. Daryl and I have always had an affinity—similar interests, backgrounds and friends. The difference is Daryl is a genius of design.

His sense of proportion and ability to blend materials and matter are only possessed by the greatest architects. His list of projects—from the famous Southern Stand at the Melbourne Cricket Ground, to the High Court and National Library in Canberra, to his own unique houses in Victoria

Portholes link Reception to the Bar in the Arrivals Hall Building.
OPPOSITE: All the children's pools are protected from the sun by gigantic shade structures.

The Eco-Cabins are surrounded by the natural beauty of the Australian bush.

Never say Never

Even the Pool Filtration Shed on Spa Island has its own beauty.

and in Australian Embassies worldwide—illustrate this gift in abundance. Daryl has won numerous Architectural and Design Awards in Australia and internationally (I was in the audience when he was acclaimed International Architect of the Year by the Royal British Society of Architects in London).

He made a perfect job of interpreting what I wanted for Cannons, our Health and Fitness Club in London. Over there, with a few rough sketches on transparent paper, Daryl solved within minutes of my briefing him what I had been trying to achieve, over a frustrating eight months, with two different firms of British architects.

It was the same with Couran Cove. He immediately understood Helen's and my enthusiastic scribblings and showed us how it could all come together. Within a week or so we had produced the basic conceptual plan and designs of the **Marine Resort**—the core of the Couran Cove dream.

Daryl's Brisbane office, led by David Trott, was stretched administratively with other projects—the main two being the new grandstand at the Gabba (football ground) and the Brisbane Hospital extension. For the design of the Eco-Cabin within the **Nature Resort**, we searched far and wide and discovered a dedicated Environmental Architect, Graham Osborne, down the coast in Byron Bay.

Graham had a long history of involvement with environmental projects and had developed an Eco-Cabin prototype which seemed ideal for our purposes. It is these Eco-Cabins which make the whole project economically feasible.

OPPOSITE: *The central boardwalk is the heart of the Maritime Village.*

I have to admit I had some problems convincing our overseas Directors of their appeal to Australians. Their experience was that the two types of Resorts, Marine and Nature, didn't mix and we should opt for one or the other. This may be correct for the rest of the world but I believe Australians are different, and this was a difficult message to communicate.

I know of no other people so unimpressed by social, racial, religious or financial status. In my experience you often find millionaires, eminent judges and politicians sharing camp sites, fishing boats or golf courses with wharf labourers and truck drivers. What counts is what sort of a bloke you are, rather than where you come from, what you are worth, or what you do for a crust.

With the unique opportunities the site offered, I believed combining these two quite different, yet complementary, types of accommodation would work. And the bookings and guests' comments to date seem to prove this.

With Graham Osborne came his wife Sally, a colour consultant and lecturer in the topic at the University of NSW in Armidale. Her excellent choice of subtle colours, to complement the earthy tones of the flora surrounding the Eco-Cabins, matched Helen's ideas and personal preferences. Together they created a superb blend of furniture and interiors for the Eco-Cabins, as Helen did for the core Hotel Buildings and Apartments with Daryl Jackson's Interior Designers.

In the UK, Helen had done wonders with the interiors and the gardens of the manor house (Combe Grove Manor built in 1712) that we converted into a Country Club Hotel

FOLLOWING PAGES: *The 192 Marine Apartments overlook either the boat harbour or the interior lagoon.*

The kitchens of the Eco-Cabins look out into the surrounding nature reserves.

OPPOSITE: ***The Kites Nest Eco-Cabin has an upper storey nesting among the treetops.***

in Bath. Here, in an almost diametrically contrasting setting, she had risen to the occasion wonderfully. My wife is not a person who compromises easily. Everything has to be perfect, right down to the smallest detail, from the colours and the framing of every painting in every building in the Resort, to each unit's salt and pepper shakers. All have to match, to blend, and to meet her exacting standards. The result is as near to perfect as is humanly possible.

One essential that I insisted on in the design of the hotel rooms (the Marine Apartments), which are the only accommodation units in the entire Resort to share floor/ceiling structures and common walls, was a complete elimination of any transfer of noise between units. Consequently hundreds of thousands of additional dollars were spent to separate acoustically the side-by-side and floor-and-ceiling structures.

Under each floor is a 250 mm special corked cavity which absorbs all sounds. A fire-rated barrier is also provided by two layers of special 13 mm plasterboard fixed to a furring channel. This adds to the acoustic barrier. Similarly, there is not one, but two, side-by-side partitions with 50 mm thick acoustic insulation, a double stud wall system and a further layer of 16 mm fire-grade plasterboard. (A graphic realisation of this work is seen here.)

Now the Resort is open the practical proof is evident. Those extra building works have proven to be a good investment as there is no noise transferred from adjoining apartments be they next door, above or below.

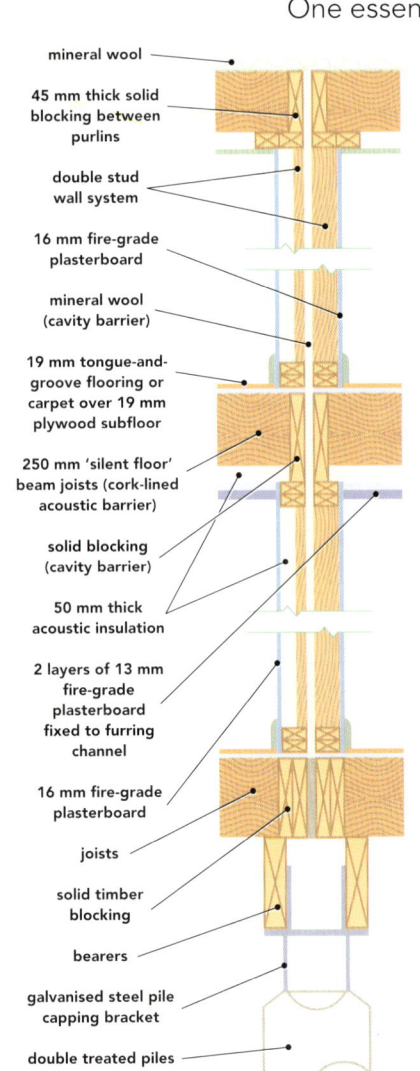

A section through a fire-rated wall of the Marine Apartments shows the fire-resistant and sound-control measures used.

OPPOSITE: **The Marine Apartments, overlooking the lagoon, greet the morning sun.**

The Architecture

Daryl Jackson

South Stradbroke Island is a remarkable piece of southern Queensland coastline. Its detachment from, yet proximity to, the Gold Coast mainland provides significant values and challenges for the visitor.

The Broadwater and the inlet to Couran Cove offer safe sailing and an intimate waterway and the surf beach, with its uninterrupted dunal foreshore, stretches north and south to meet the far horizon. Between these waters there is mature native bushland with secret pieces of tropical rainforest—a special treat. Within this setting the Maritime Village Hotel is perched, touching the land lightly as a gull might use its legs on the beach.

All the buildings are designed to convey an attitude towards and for the landscape values, to infiltrate the bush, to hover over the water of the new cove outline and, more particularly, to make connections via the long jetty which forms a promenade between the inner and outer lagoon. Being on the water is the special quality offered by this Resort. It is the essential point of difference to life at home or in the majority of hotels.

The buildings possess a character that recognisably belongs to Queensland, deploying white corrugated iron, saw texture stained timber, painted weatherboard, plantation louvre panels and batten sunshades in a number of colours and combinations.

PREVIOUS PAGES: 'The buildings possess a character that recognisably belongs to Queensland.' Daryl Jackson

The spectacular boardwalk connects the Arrivals Complex and Spa Island with its restaurant, pools and recreation activities.

OPPOSITE: Heading back to the Arrivals Hall from Spa Island.

Bringing it all Together

This is regional, maritime architecture at its best, exploiting shadows cast by the subtropical light, allowing the sky-water reflection to lap against the pier structure on which the units are built.

There are differences of scale—between the deep verandahed loggia of the dining/recreation/conference pavilions and the smaller verandahs on each of the houses and between the Marina Arrivals pier and the personalised jetties attached to each waterfront dwelling.

As with maritime buildings anywhere there is a sensitive adherence to principles of structure and to a limited use of primary materials. These elements combine to form a coherent village atmosphere where, due to the consistency of approach, each building contributes to the whole and the overall impression is strengthened.

The Marine Apartments and Beachfront Lodges contribute to the aesthetics with colours of white and blue, yellow-ochre and blue-grey, grey-green, red and weathered hardwood—like a run of original bathing boxes.

Each accommodation unit has a view. Many sit out on the water (as in a boatshed) with outdoor terraces and jetties. The interiors are high gloss, cool, crisp and white, with vibrant colour in soft furnishings and curtains. Polished hardwood floors, grey-green carpet, and marble and tile surfaces highlight the quality and ensure visual comfort.

Marine Apartments are grouped in blocks of four or eight, with all rooms facing the water and sun. Upper levels look across the man-made harbour towards the Broadwater, seen

All balconies of Marine Apartments provide the perfect retreat with a water view.

OPPOSITE: **The spectacular separated sun roof adds a stylised shade cover to the apartments without inhibiting the cooling sea breezes.**

ACCOMMODATION

Marine Resort

192 MARINE APARTMENTS
Studio & extra 1-bedroom

50 BEACHFRONT LODGES
1, 2 & 3-bedroom

25 BROADWATER VILLAS
3 & 4-bedroom

Nature Resort

278 ECO-CABINS
1-bedroom Pandanus
2-bedroom Cottonwood
3-bedroom Kites Nest

3 WILDERNESS LODGES
6 units (32 beds)

Ocean Beach Camp

100 TENTS
and associated facilities

---

through the masts of assembled yachts sheltering within the Marina. They have high ceilings and skylights to maximise natural light and ventilation.

Designed as a studio or with an extra separate bedroom, which allows the living area to remain open for entertaining during the day, they have the potential to sleep more should visitors choose to stay. Each has a large covered balcony some 3 metres deep which is designed as an outdoor room, to catch the breezes, experience the waterways and connect to the harbour or Spa Island. Large bathrooms are luxuriously finished with marble and a compact kitchen enables light meals and breakfasts to be prepared.

Beachfront Lodges are designed to be flexible. Rooms may be added, sleepouts extended, viewing lofts incorporated and internal walls rearranged. As the family grows, so too can the holiday accommodation. A fully equipped kitchen and a luxuriously appointed bathroom complete the dwelling.

The Lodges are paired each side of a land bridge connecting to the tidal lagoon and the harbour. A generous living area opens up to a large deck overlooking the water. Privacy is assured via screen walls. These have an enjoyable boatshed holiday approach of being able to live over or adjacent to the water—it's all part of the fun.

As with the Conference and Reception Centre buildings, a carefully developed system of coloured weatherboards, white windows and charcoal trim characterises the architecture.

A series of two-storey Broadwater Villas occupy the water's edge of the canal to the south of the Maritime Village. Each has the opportunity for a personalised boat mooring or anchorage, just beyond the front door. Other Villas are placed to the western edge of the Resort where views from upper level living/dining rooms and cantilevered decks are quite spectacular.

These Villas consist of three bedrooms, a bathroom and a games room on a lower deck with the first floor occupied by kitchen, living/dining, main bedroom suite and bathroom. As family housing, this mixture of rooms offers a significant variation of occupancy and amenity.

As with the Maritime Village, a consistency of materials and colours ensures integration of the designs into the overall picture.

Spa Island is the centrepiece of the inner lagoon, connected to the reception and restaurant area by a footbridge. It enables children and adults to share in a series of wading and bathing areas, spas and a 25-metre 10-lane lap swimming pool.

Shade-giving umbrellas and a large flowing canopy offer protection from the sun. One can have a massage there or a delightful al fresco lunch at the Spa Island Cafe which is set within the swimming pool complex.

FOLLOWING PAGES: Spa Island is the idyllic water retreat for the whole family.

The boardwalk outside the shops and restaurant provides plenty of space for guests to stroll and chat.

The Arrivals Hall has large verandahs attached to each side of the Bar and first-class main Restaurant—dining outside overlooking the lagoon or the cove brings an urbanity that one detects in the street life of St Kilda, Bondi or Noosa. Even the interior dining area can open up to the verandahs so everyone gets to be part of the picture.

For conferences, club visits, educators and environmental enthusiasts, a further range of facilities is included. The upper level seminar rooms and breakfast meeting areas overlook the cove and the lagoon, with spectacular views of the Broadwater also. The area below is a multipurpose space for a large General Store and kiosk.

With Ron Clarke in charge, there is no lack of opportunities for a healthy lifestyle. Athletics, squash, tennis, sailing, wind surfing, swimming, lawn bowls, boules (petanque), bocce, bush walking, bird watching and running are all possible, carefully designed so anyone can participate at a comfortable level that suits interest and ability.

Surfing at the pristine, though handsomely untouched, dune beach is a contrasting experience. One can feel alone on this eastern edge of the island and only the great Pacific Ocean knows you are there.

High above the dune there is a Surf Club restaurant known as the Oceanman Surf Club. The views are astonishing and on the wide verandah the company and food are intended to match. The beach is a 20-minute

Children, seen here climbing the 'Eiffel Tower' rope structure, love the range of equipment in their huge playground.

OPPOSITE: *Spa Island's 25-metre pool is heated all year round and caters for both serious and social swimmers.*

Bringing it all Together

walk through the bush on a gravel path. But it can also be a shorter bicycle ride or electric buggy experience.

At Couran Cove Resort, each house or holiday unit has special qualities, but they are all designed to complement neighbouring residences and the group of buildings that are the focal point of the Maritime Village. They all form part of a whole, yet are themselves whole. The overall theme of individuality is protected by the compatibility of a sensitive, yet thoroughly related and enjoyable, holiday area.

Gold Coast City Council lifeguards protect swimmers in the surf, all day, every day of the year.

Just as Spa Island permits every opportunity for civilised recreation, a walk or jog through the bush to the Surf Club and the remoteness of the Pacific edge provides a natural contrast. Here the wilderness of wind on water evokes the healthy contrast of being detached yet paradoxically in contact with a sense of values, which allows the natural world and human activity to come together and be celebrated.

Set apart from the Gold Coast by water, Couran Cove has a distinctive difference where the eco-system remains largely intact. Care in tree retention, use of appropriate materials and dunal beach protection are the key aspects of relatively new values for tourism projects, where preservation and sustainability are important to the Australian landscape.

As Ron Clarke would say, 'Couran Cove is designed to stimulate all our senses. Maximum enjoyment at every level, for all age groups is on offer, we are a hotel with a relaxed recreational focus that is active and passive, urbane and intelligent.'

OPPOSITE: The eastern surf beach is nature's paradise.

The Eco-Cabins

Graham Osborne

On my first visit to the site of Couran Cove Resort I experienced a remarkable sense of removal from the artificial world of the Gold Coast mainland. The naturalness of the island, only a short ride across the water, where peace and quiet and nature reign, enveloped me with a pleasant sense of isolation—a somewhere-miles-away feeling. My challenge was to retain and impart this feeling to the design expression of the architecture.

The Eco-Cabins were challenging because I had to resist the temptation to make them 'like home' and have them reflect a fun holiday atmosphere in the 'as nature would have it' ethos of the Resort.

Consequently they have been designed for lightweight minimal impact and disturbance to the site, and to keep natural vegetation and fauna eco-systems intact. The external colours blend with the site and maintain visual integrity.

All three cabin designs—Pandanus, Cottonwood and Kites Nest—have a feeling of casual openness. Their design ensures that the surrounding bushland encompasses and feels part of the living space with screened verandah areas and often enclosed trees as part of the deck area, yet at the same time providing protection from the elements to ensure comfort.

The design and colours of the Eco-Cabins ensure harmony with the surrounding bush.

OPPOSITE: A Cottonwood Eco-Cabin is framed by the majestic form of a saw-leaf banksia (Banksia serrata).

The louvre windows provide ventilation in the summer.

Relaxing on the deck of an Eco-Cabin is an insect-free experience.

A combination of fixed and roll-away insect screens and shadecloth under decking to the top of the pergola complete the insect-free environment. Polycarbonate roofing cleverly disguised above the grey shadecloth gives filtered light and weather protection as well as reflecting added daylight through the overhead louvre banks.

The Eco-Cabins are designed to breathe naturally, by venting warmer air through upper clerestory windows and allowing cross ventilation of natural air flow and cooling sea breezes. Being built above ground, on wooden pilings, also aids air circulation. Natural wool insulation maintains warmth in winter and coolness in summer.

Timbers of bamboo origin, such as 'Plyboo' bamboo floors, as well as certified sustainable plantation timbers were used for construction and internal finishes, with materials being selected for ease of upkeep.

The use of environmental colour themes provides each precinct with an identity as well as harmonising each building with its natural setting. The use of deeper neutral external finishes integrates the Eco-Cabins with the bush and

simulates the banksia, whose dark green leaves provide a protective barrier from the sun. The light creamy underside of the leaves creates a cool and light environment which has been replicated in the interiors.

Bringing it all Together

Colours, manufactured specially for Couran Cove, were selected over a full year of detailed research and analysis from a palette which included small bursts of intense seasonal colour contrasting to the consistently unified background colour—a variety of shades of yellow-green.

The interior colours and finishes are as natural as function allowed. The principal finish on internal walls is a 'wood wash' (water-based limewash), partly derived from cow's milk, which gives a unified light treatment for the natural wood linings.

The choice of products used in the furnishings emphasises natural finishes at all times, such as hemp fabric, pure wool blankets and maize matting. Against this natural background, the paintings and prints of local Gold Coast artist, Ian Tremewen, provide spectacular contrasting bursts of colour.

Energy efficient lighting and appliances were used throughout. During the day the verandah roof acts as a light shelf to reflect light and air across the curved ceiling into the interior which not only creates a greater sense of space, but avoids the need for artificial lighting during the day. Solar hot water units are installed on all cabins.

To maintain this natural atmosphere, roads and paths disguise the service routes; meters are replaced by pulse meter technology; and wires or antennae on buildings are refreshingly absent.

FOLLOWING PAGES: *The Eco-Cabins are designed to blend into the natural environment.*

Natural products, such as bamboo floors and sustainable timbers, are used in the Eco-Cabins.

Living the Dream

Ron Clarke

A cautious agile wallaby (Macropus agilis) peers through the vegetation towards the observer.

A major feature of the planned layout of the Resort is the manner in which we have been able to concentrate on establishing a hub or core for the central activities, with the remaining facilities and accommodation radiating out in a series of concentric semicircles.

Helen and I instinctively sketched a rough plan which followed these principles because the natural features of the site dictated that this was the way to go. Other resorts we visited seemed to lack a 'heart', a central focus, or a 'water well' as one guest later described it (in Biblical times, the water well of a village was the central meeting place, where gossip was exchanged, and villagers chatted and schemed).

The forest floor provides bursts of colour from many different Australian fungi.
OPPOSITE: Take only photographs, leave only footprints.

Daryl Jackson, our Architect, endorsed our thoughts. Each fishing village and each town has a core—a gathering point, he told us as he converted our pencilled outlines into firm, boldly pencilled plans. We should have a walkway along the weir where the Resort's citizens (guests) can stroll and meet and talk, where the store and the cafes and the restaurants are located. People can meet there, while away the time, eat, shop or book activities.

Uncommon locally, the giant water lily (Nymphaea gigantea) can be found in the Resort's ponds.

PREVIOUS PAGES: *Yet another spectacular sunset over the Resort.*

This interesting and delicate tick orchid (Dendrobium linguiforme) produces small white flowers in summer.

As our axis we had two points of reference. The precious glade of old mango trees appealed to us as the perfect location for an outdoor wooden chapel and relaxation area which could be the natural extension of the central boardwalk, and the majestic blue gum that we saved (by extending a small isthmus into the lagoon and rock walling around it to offset any penetration of the tree's roots by the lagoon's salt water). This perfect example of an Australian tree, its silver trunk and branches lit at night, could also provide a spectacular sight for guests as they walked up the arrival ramp. These were the parameters we set for Daryl and his team to site the core of the Resort.

Then within the next circle we wanted to have all the sports and recreational activities (including the nature and rainforest walks) thus locating these between the Maritime Village and the Eco-Cabins set in the forest. This middle circle of facilities, which surrounds the core of the Marine Resort, works perfectly. All the jogging/walking/cycling trails start from here. These exceptional facilities, which form the substantial recreation and activity part of the Resort, are in a wonderful setting and provide a buffer zone between the two areas of accommodation.

Of course we couldn't rearrange the surf beach so that becomes a destination to the east of the Resort—a 2-kilometre walk, bike ride or road train journey away. As well as the Pacific Ocean, this outer circle of serenity provides wilderness areas, nature trails and the Broadwater.

It all works rather well.

OPPOSITE: **The Livistona australis rainforest almost envelops its visitors.**

175

Living the Dream

Colourful insects abound throughout the rainforest, consuming leaves and timber and providing food for other wildlife.

OPPOSITE: *The dimpled bark of the familiar beach resident, pandanus (Pandanus tectorius).*

FOLLOWING PAGES: *A group of black-winged stilts (Himantopus himantopus) at sunset.*

The striped marsh frog (Limnodynastes peronii) is a common inhabitant of the Resort's western coast.

PAGES 180–181: The developing flowers of the saw-leaf banksia (Banksia serrata).

OPPOSITE: A rich ground cover of climbing maidenhair fern (Lygodium microphyllum) and sedge (Isolepis nodosa) can be found adjacent to wetland areas.

183

Living the Dream

OPPOSITE: *Low tide and sunset make for spectacular photography along the vast western beach.*

The grey mangrove (Avicennia marina) binds the sand together and protects the foreshore with its visible and extensive root system.

PAGES 188–189: *The fragile eastern foredunes are held together by the twining stems of the beach spinifex (Spinifex sericeus).*

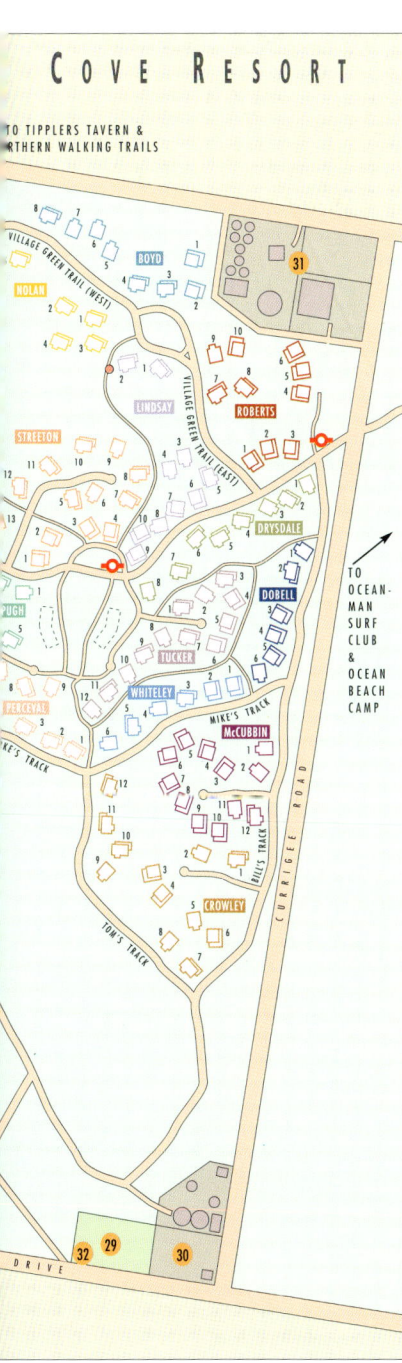

The Team — Consultants & Contractors

A1 Filtration – Water Treatment Plant Contractors
Bill Doyle

Action Shopfitters
Martin Cole

Airvac – RSM Pty Ltd
Geoff Radinoff
David Saunders

Australian Conservation Foundation
Peter Farrell

Bennett & Bennett
Lyn Bennett
Peter Ireland

Bill Adams Tiling
Bill Adams

Bruce Lemcke Engineering – Structural Engineer
Bruce Lemcke

Christopher West Plumbing
Geoff Christopher
Shane Porter
Jason Curico

Coastline – Carpentry, Plasterboard Partitions & Ceilings
Neville Johnston
Col Partridge
Markus Kraft

Daryl Jackson Architects
Daryl Jackson
David Trott
Gilbert Gouveia
Jen Smit

Department of Environment
Richard Birt (Senior Environmental Officer)

Douglas Partners – Hydrologist
Bron Smolski

Edward Smith & Associates – Fire Consultants
Edward Smith

Encon Tanks – Supplier of Potable & Effluent Storage Tanks
Darrin Drew

Enviroflow – Sewage Treatment Plant Suppliers
Daniel Bergade

Everton Excavation
Daryl Anderson

Focus – Environmental Consultants
Jane Stanley

Food Service Design – Kitchen Consultants
Terry Brennan

Funnell Hydraulics – Hsydraulics Engineers
Paul Funnell
Paul Jack

Gibson Quai & Associates – Communications Engineers
Peter de Haas
Dennis Stockwell

G James Glass & Aluminium
Klaus Schrader
Robert De Graaf

Glenzeil – Construction Management
Ken Jones
Geoff Rose
Mark Cowie
Steve White

Grummitt Planning – Town Planners
Noel Grummitt

Inka Constructions
Peter Margetts

Integrated Energy Services – Energy Consultants
Frank Barram

Jondalar Pty Ltd – Carpentry
Ken Kamyilmaz
Dev Kamyilmaz

Kim Fulton & Associates – Surveyors
Kim Fulton

Lincolne Scott – Electrical & Mechanical Engineers
John Peacock
Roger Hawkins

Louise Saunders – Artwork
Louise Saunders

Malcolm Newton – Builder (Eco-Cabins)
Malcolm Newton

Marlandecol Technologies
Adam Slijderink

Master Kelwin Vinyl & Carpets
Jeff Cameron

Measurement Engineering
Chris Hoey
Rod Lougheed

Neumann Contractors
David Smith

Nullarbor Prevention
Bill Wilcock

O'Donnell Griffin – Electrical & Communication Contractors
Bob Roche
Phil Craig

Origen Architecture (formerly Arkishop)
Graham Osborne
Sally Osborne (colours)

OSMOflo – Water Treatment Plant Engineer
Marc Fabig

Pacific Pier & Pontoon – Marine Constructions
Bill Bourke

RACE Airconditioning
Ian Robbie

Retail Display Shopfitters
David McGregor

Rider Hunt – Quantity Surveyors
Stuart Rayner

Ronstan – Balustrade Rigging
Peter Dowdney

Selective Plumbing
Miles Nathan

SE Power Equipment – Power Station Suppliers
Stuart Pringle
Rob Ientile

Sinclair Knight Merz – Consulting Engineers
Wayne Currey
Peter Griffin
Phil Perkins
David Fallon

Smith & Wallace – Engineers
Phillip Wallace

Spancrete – Formwork & Concreting Contractors
Jim Carston

Stamwell & Stanford – Piling Contractors
Rob Stanford

Stegbar – Mirrors & Shower Screens
Roger Slack

Stoddart Metal – Kitchen Equipment
Steve Osten

Superior Jetty & Pontoon Constructions
Greg Goody

Surfside Pool – Pool Constructors
Ian Hodge

Taringa Steel – Steel Fabrication
Chris Scott
Dereck Bolton

Tema Engineers – Coordination & Design of Dynasand Unit
Yee Yeng Chee

Tremewen Water Colour & Design – Artwork
Ian Tremewen
Jennifer Maroney
Vern Tremewen

Tripart Painting – Painting Contractors
Col MacArthur
Paul Pring

Vision Cabinet – Joinery
David Sukar

Watpac – Builder
Garry Rossow
Phil Corcoran
Chris Stanley
Nick Halsey
Brian Gildea
Gary Gisik
Wayne Rowe

The Team — Resort Staff

Sue Aitken
Administrative Coordinator – Conventions

Jason Alderson
Pantry Service Attendant

David Allcock
Tradesman/Electrician

Elizabeth Allen
Personal Assistant – Director of Sales & Marketing

Casanne Alpen
Cost Controller

Mike Anderson
Food & Beverage Attendant (Food Van)

Hayley Anthony
Groundsperson

Michael Arthy
Groundsperson/Waste Management Team Member

Michael Askin
Grounds Manager

Jefferson Bacon
Waste Management Team Leader

Scott Baguley
Food & Beverage Attendant

Theresa Bartells
Demi Chef

Gregory Bax
Assistant Grounds Manager

Malcolm Beechey
Receptionist – Island

Robert Benze
Assistant Manager – Housekeeping

Jacques Beylacq
Island Store & Stewarding Manager

Kevin Bingham
Team Leader

Craig Bingley
Team Member

Michael Boyd
Assistant Manager – Check In/Valet/Reception

Norm Brown
Rooms Handyperson

Jacky Buzaglo
Guest Services Officer – Communications

Stephen Byrne
IT Support

Michael Campbell
IT Support (6 months)

Scott Campbell
Accountant

Tania Canale
Assistant Night Manager

Nigel Canterbury
Houseperson

David Cearns
Sports Facility Manager

Darren Chapman
Guest Services Officer – Baggage – Runaway Bay

Karl Cherwin
Forklift Driver/Pantry

Pam Chisholm
Communications Team Leader

Helen Clarke
Interiors

Nicolas Clarke
Sports Attendant

Ron Clarke
Chief Executive

Troy Clunies-Ross
Guest Services Officer – Baggage – Runaway Bay

Larry Cockerton
Houseperson

Barbara Collins
Guest Services Officer – Communications

Dan Collins
Assistant Recreation Manager

Jenny Collins
Room Attendant

Grant Cook
Chef

Rachel Cooke
Outlet Manager

John Corcoran
Chef de Partie

David Coward
Steward

Denita Cragg
Human Resources Administration/Recruitment

Denise Crofts
Team Member

Tanya Cross
Sandwich Hand

Mary Cullum
Room Attendant – Night

Daniel Cundy
Groundsperson

Gaylene Dale
Runaway Bay Terminal Team Leader

Charles Daoud
Food & Beverage Manager

Harry Davies
Groundsperson

Anthony Davis
Team Leader

Lyndon Discombe
Rooms Division Manager/FOM

Scott Douglas
Mechanic

Jim Downey
Consultant

James Doyle
Room Attendant

Corrine Duncan
Room Attendant

Gus Duncan
Water Sports Attendant

Mike Dwyer
Director of Sales & Marketing

Patrick Dyer
Gymnasium Manager

Danielle Egan
Administration/Team Leader

Don Elmer
Spa Island & Pools Manager

Chuck Feeney
IPG

Sue Filetti
Room Attendant

Paula Fisher
Reservation Clerk

Sheryl Fitzgerald
Sandwich Hand

Lesli Fletcher
Secretary – General Manager

Warwick Forbes
Coomera Stores Clerk

Penny Forrester
Food & Beverage Attendant

Dennis Fountain
Operations Manager

Jason Fountain
Guest Services Officer – Baggage – Runaway Bay

Matthew Fuller
Chef

Peter Gannon
Maintenance Coordinator

Vince Garrett
Tradesman/Electrician

Paul Gayfer
Purchasing Officer

Peter Gillies
Manager – Hospitality

Sandra Gillies
Kids Club – Coordinator

Bob Goldman
IPG

Mike Gorrie
Financial Controller

Werner Graef
IPG

Sharron Griffiths
Human Resources Officer

Douglas Hague-Smith
Chef

Tony Harris
Rooms Handyperson

Jane Harse
Team Leader

Scott Hayden
Security Manager

Michael Heidemann
Mechanical Team Leader

Adam Hellyer
Groundsperson/Waste Management Team Member

Craig Henkelmann
Sous Chef

Patricia Higgins
Accounts Payable/Trust Account

Wayne Higgins
Bike Maintenance

Zane Holt
Banquet Services Manager

Nicole Hoy
Food & Beverage Attendant

Helen Hughes
Team Leader

Samantha Hughes
Sports Attendant

Stewart Hulme
Night Porter

John Jacobs
Rooms Handyperson

Glen Johnson
Team Leader – Spa Island Chef

David Jones
Chef de Partie

Rebecca Jones
Guest Services Officer – Baggage – Runaway Bay

The Team

Kathleen Kelly
Credit Manager/AR Clerk

Anne Kinnane
Public Relations Manager

Matt Kirk
Apprentice

John Kremmer
Island Fire & Safety Manager

Matthew Kruger
Houseperson

Kris Kyle
Guest Services Officer – Baggage – Runaway Bay

Joanna Larsen
Room Attendant

Donella Latham
Outlet Manager

Darren Lee
Pantry Service Attendant

Scott Lewis
Guest Services Officer – Rooms

Frank Liberatore
Tradesman/Electrician

Luc Lignieres
Pastry Chef

John Lindsay
Groundsperson

Kirk Links
Guest Services Officer – Sports

Keith Lipke
Steward

Megan Lloyd
Guest Services Officer – Communications

Brendan Long
Recreation Manager

Nicholas Luke
Groundsperson

Tony Maher
Guests Services Officer – Baggage

Sean Mallard
Houseperson

Kylie Mapleson
Outlet Manager

David Martin
Train Driver

Todd McClelland
Guest Services Officer – Baggage – Runaway Bay

Alastair McCracken
General Manager

Kathy McDaid
Sales Secretary

Susan McRostie
Credit Manager/AR Clerk

Oscar Miel
Chef

Anne Millis
Sales Manager – National

Angela Morrison
Sales Coordinator

John Morrison
Rooms Handyman

Erin Moston
Reservations Team Leader

Madonna Moulds
Guest Services Officer – Rooms

Terry Murphy
Assistant Operations Manager

Paul Neilson
Receptionist – Island

Jarrod Norman
Chef de Partie

Megan Norris
Food & Beverage Attendant

Bradley Nye
Night Porter

Leah Nye
Human Resources Administration/ Payroll

Simon O'Brien
Acting Team Leader

Lee O'Connell
Reservation Clerk – Runaway Bay

Danielle Oddy
Total Living Centre – Manager/Secretary

Jill Ogden
Runaway Bay Terminal Manager

Dowel O'Reilly
Guest Services/Handyperson

Tammy O'Sullivan
Nursery Propagator

Lois Paterson
Accounts Payable

Kylie Patrick
Trainee Guides

Lynda Peacock
Director of Human Resources

Matthew Peel
Apprentice

Angelina Perez
Room Attendant

Joanne Pinel
Team Leader

Stephen Plumridge
IT Manager

Lainie Poon
Assistant Manager – Rooms

Robert Predebon
Laundry Attendant Coomera Store

John Press
Coomera Stores Clerk

Chris Pullen
Team Leader

Kim Rabelink
Apprentice

Vincent Ras
Steward

Mike Reardon
Site Planner

Shari Renwick
Food & Beverage Attendant

Susan Rodger
Sales Manager – Conference

Matthew Rowe
Chef

Clinton Salisbury
Coomera Stores Clerk

Darren Saxon
Receptionist – Island

Kathie Sayed
Food & Beverage Attendant (Food Van)

Robert Schruf
Guest Services Officer – Rooms

Scott Sellens
Team Member

Libby Sharp
Housekeeping Manager

Laura Sherman-Hayes
Trainee Guides

Monica Sietz
Food & Beverage Attendant

David Small
Pantry Service Attendant

David Smith
Director

Julie Smith
Room Attendant

Paul Smith
Ropes Course

Rob Smith
Mechanical Handyman/Fire Officer

Bradley Smyth
General Cashier/Income Audit

Lara Solyma
Groundsperson

Robert Stanley
Works Supervisor

Michele Stevens
Assistant Manager – Rooms

Melissa Stevenson
Team Leader

Natalie Stevenson
Food & Beverage/Sports Attendant

Gillian Taylor
Personal Assistant – Chief Executive

Damian ten Bohmer
Banquets & Conventions Manager

Yon Tesch
Groundsperson

Cindy Tickle
Team Leader

Guy Tickle
Harbour Master

Jim Toll
Purchasing Manager

Scott Toohey
Manager – Environmental Department

Thomas Vaughan
Team Member

Wendy Walker
Team Leader

Rebecca Waller
Sports Attendant

Kevin Ward
Forklift Driver

Paul Ward
Nursery Team Leader

Mat Waters
Executive Chef

Angus Westaway
Steward

Michael White
Steward

Jesse Wilkinson
Groundsperson

Mark Wilkinson
Assistant Director – Food & Beverage

Allan Wong
Steward

Michael Woodbry
Project Manager

Lesley Woodger
Reception – Runaway Bay

Peter Woolley
Project Manager

James Wright
Chef

Sally Wright
Guest Services Officer – Rooms

Jerry Wunderlich
IPG

Peter Yorston
Houseperson

Jamie Young
Activities Coordinator

Martin Ziviani
Guest Services Officer – Rooms

Index

Aborigines
    and development 15
    on South Stradbroke Island 57–8, 62
acid sulfate soils 15, 81–2, 90–1, 98
    treatment of 91
agriculture 63, 99, 119
airconditioning 126
architecture 148–9, 150–61, 162–5
    appropriate 16, 119
    Daryl Jackson designs 49
    insulation 126
    maritime 153
    solar design 126
    see also building materials, Eco-Cabins, Marine Apartments
Arrivals Complex 139, 150, 151, 158, 184–5
Australian Conservation Foundation (ACF) 82, 98, 114
Avicennia marina 25, 64–5, 78–9, 183

bandicoot, northern brown 114
Banksia
    integrifolia 15, 30, 32, 43, 57, 59
    serrata 5, 52, 107, 163, 180–1
banksia 58, 86, 164
    coastal 15, 30, 32, 43, 57, 59
    saw-leaf 5, 52, 107, 163, 180–1
Barram, Frank 124
bats 15
Beach Protection Authority 72
Beachfront Lodges 153, 154
bees 94
bibliography 191
birds 15, 27
    see also by name
boardwalk
    central 87, 141, 150, 155, 172
    elevated rainforest *front cover inset*, 100–5, 115
Boat Marina 56
Boiga irregularis 107
bridge proposal 70
Broadwater 25, 45, 56, 68, 98, 150, 172, 184–5
Broadwater beach 19, 182
Broadwater Villas 154, 155
building materials 150,165
    barging 15
    for Eco-Cabins 164
    sustainable timber 119
    sympathetic 16
buildings see architecture
    see also Beachfront Lodges, Broadwater Villas, Eco-Cabins, Marine Apartments
bungwall 58
bush tucker 89
butterfly
    common crow 94
    native 94

Caamano, Tom 88
cabbage-tree palm 10, 38, 39, 39, 58, 58, 73, 98,107

Cambus Wallace 69
canal development 70, 71
Cannons Health and Fitness Club, London 40, 51, 140
Carpobrotus glaucescens 49
Casuarina
    equisetifolia 23, 89, 98
    glauca 41
cattle 62, 99, 119
    removal 72
chemicals 94, 121
chlorine 121
Clarke, Helen 23, 34
    Combe Grove Manor, Bath 40, 143
    Eco-Cabins 143, 146
Clarke, Ron 34, 35
    schooling 50, 50–1
    typical summer holiday 23, 26
    World Games, Helsinki 16
Clarke family 23, 23–30, 24, 26, 34
Clayton's Lake 12–13, 48, 72, 99, 120, 120
Colus hirudinosus 81
Combe Grove Manor, Bath 40, 40, 143
composting process 131, 132, 133
Conference and Reception Centre 154, 158
Conservation Park 77
conservationists 15, 87
    see also eco-tourism, environment
consultants and contractors see Couran Cove Resort
Cooling, Beth 88
cottonwood tree 58
'Couran' 31, 66
Couran Cove 150
    agriculture at 63
Couran Cove Resort 35, 56, 71, 170–1
    consultants and contractors 185
    Daryl Jackson designs 51
    designed for Australian families 53
    development 139–65
    map 184–5
    site 15–19
    staff 186–7
    vegetation map 98
Couran Cove Resort Environmental Research Trust see Environmental Research Trust Fund
Currigee 56, 62, 63, 66
    bridge proposal 70
    entertainment at 77
    school at 72
Cyathea cooperi 17

Dacelo novaeguineae 33
Dandenongs 24, 30, 34
Dendrobium linguiforme 172
diesel fuel 124
dragonfly 72
Dromana 24, 26, 30
Dux's Mooring 56, 72
Dynasand filter 133, 133

Eco-Cabins 15, 99, 116–17, 139, 162–5,162, 165, 166–7, 172
    Cottonwood 154, 162, 163

design 140
gas heating 125
kitchens 143
Kites Nest 15, 142, 154, 162
Pandanus 154, 162
solar hot water 126, 165
eco-tourism 108, 113–14
    sustainability of 161
'Eiffel Tower' rope structure 158
electricity see Energy Management Control System
elkhorn fern 74–5, 83
Elsey, Bernard 70
Energy Management Control System 108, 124–7, 127
    savings 125, 126
    see also power usage
Enviroflow 132, 133, 133
environment 15, 107–37
    see also landscape, pest control, rehabilitation, waste management, weed control
Environmental Education Centre 72
Environmental Research Trust Fund 89, 125
erosion 71
Essendon 24, 24, 50
eucalypt woodland 2–3, 98, 99
Eucalyptus
    tereticornis 8
    tessellaris 31, 53
Euploea core 94

Farrell, Peter 82, 88
Ferny Creek 34–5, 35, 35, 45
fire 99
    green fire break 133
fog spraying 134
forest 66, 128–9, 168
    see also eucalypt woodland, mangroves, rainforest
four-wheel-drive vehicles 53, 108, 113
Fraser Island 120
Frog Lake 94
frogs, native 94
    striped marsh frog 178
    see also tree frog
fungi 168

Gardner, Richard 69
gas see LPG
General Store 132, 158
generators 125, 127
    monitoring 124
Goenpul people 57
Gold Coast 49, 56, 150, 162
Gold Coast City Council 72, 77, 81
    monitoring soil treatment 82
Gold Coast Seaway 56
    see also Southport Seaway
golf course 120
greenhouse 88
greenhouse gas emissions 124, 125
    reduced 126, 127
Griffin, Peter 81
gum 99
    'Couran' 31

forest red 8
Gum Tree Point 6–7
    blue gum 172

Hamilton Island 15
herb garden 89
High Court, Canberra 139
Himantopus himantopus 176–7
Hooker-Rex development 70, 70
horses 62
horsetail oaks 23, 89

indigenous species 81, 82, 94, 98
    revegetation cycle 95
    vegetation types 98
Integrated Energy Systems 124
Interior Designers 143
interiors and furnishings 143, 153
    for Eco-Cabins 165
Interpacific Resorts (Australia) Pty Ltd 44, 71
introduced species 87
    bees 94
    see also agriculture, cattle
Isodon macrourus 114
Isolepis nodosa 61, 179

Jackson, Daryl 49–51, 50, 139–40, 143, 169, 172
    Cannons 51
Jackson, Kay 49–51
Jacob's Well 72
jeerabing 62
Jones, Caroline 23, 35
Jumpinpin 56, 62, 62, 69

kangaroo apple 60
kingfisher, sacred 108
    see also kookaburra, laughing
Kombamerri people 57, 66
kookaburra, laughing 33

lace monitors 110–11
landscaping 114
    see also indigenous species, Native Plant Nursery, rehabilitation
Latter, Bob 63
Leiper, Glenn 88
Lifeguard Tower 56, 130, 161
light traps 134, 135
lighting 124, 125, 126, 165
Limnodynastes peronii 178
Litoria gracilenta 1, 81
Living Resources Mosquito Light Trap see light traps
Livistona australis 10, 38, 39, 39, 58, 58, 73, 98
    rainforest 98, 99, 100–5, 107, 173
lorikeets, rainbow 57, 57
LPG (liquefied petroleum gas) 124, 127, 127
    cooking 126
    dishwasher 126, 126
    heating 125
Lygodium microphyllum 179
Lyons family 69

Index

Macaranga tanarius endpapers, 44
Macropus agilis 4, 19, 45, 109, 169
maidenhair fern, climbing 179
Manager, Ben 63, 63
mango trees 172
mangroves 16, 20–1, 45, 98, 98, 112
    grey 25, 62, 64–5, 78–9, 183
    stilted 81
Maps
    Couran Cove Resort 184–5
    Couran Cove vegetation 98
    Melbourne and environs 24
    South Stradbroke Island and environs 56
Marine Apartments 9, 122–3, 139, 144–5, 147, 153–4, 154
    balconies 153
    fire resistance 146, 146
    sound control 146, 146
    sun roof 153
Marine Resort 6–7, 140, 143, 145, 154, 172, 184–5
Maritime Village 141, 155, 161, 172
    Hotel 150
Measurement Engineering 124
Meier, Leo 19
Melaleuca 42, 98
    quinquenervia 36–7, 87, 98
Melaleuca swamp 45, 98
Melbourne Cricket Ground 90
    Southern Stand, 139
Mictyris sp 23, 84–5, 119
middens 58, 184–5
mini-bats 134
Moondarewa 56, 62, 69
Moreton Bay ash 31, 53, 66
Moreton Bay Oyster Company 63
Moreton Island 57
mosquito management 94, 134, 134–5
    life cycle 135
    see also light traps
Mount, Bill 40

Nanofiltration Plant 121
National Library, Canberra 139
Native Plant Nursery 17, 87–9, 92–3, 94, 99, 119
Nature Resort 140, 143, 154, 184–5
nature walks 89, 172
Neumann Contractors 81–2, 90,
Noonuckle people 57
North Stradbroke Island 56, 57, 120
Nursery *see* Native Plant Nursery
Nymphaea gigantea 169

ocean beach *front cover*, 28–9, 39, 45, 118, 150, 158, 160, 172, 192
    rehabilitation 119
Ocean Beach Camp 154
Oceanman Surf Club 56, 120, 158
orchid
    swamp 88, 88
    tick 172
organic waste 130, 131, 132
Osborne, Graham 140, 143, 162
Osborne, Sally 143
oysters 62, 63

Pacific blue-eye fish 134, 135
Pacific Island Club 44
Pandanus tectorius 174
paperbark forests 36–7, 87
    wetland 74–5
'parrots, blue mountain' 57
pathways 114, 119
Pentatomidae 106
Persicaria elatior 88
pest control 94, 108, 119
    Eco-Cabin screens 164, 164
    mosquitoes 134–5
Phaius tankervilleae 88, 88
Picnic Point 56, 70
pigface 49
Piggott, Dave 135
pink smartweed 88
'plant a tree' experience 89
Platalea regia 113
Platycerium bifurcatum 74–5, 83
pools
    filtration shed 140
    heating 127
    shading 138, 155
    see also Spa Island
Port Phillip Bay 23, 24
Power, David 81
power usage 124, 124–7
    monitoring 127
    on-screen display 124, 125
    reduced 126

Quandamooka people 57

rainfall 120
rainforest *front cover inset*, 16, 39, 45, 51, 54–5, 80, 98, 107, 150
    elevated walk *front cover inset*, 100–105, 115
    regeneration 67
    see also Livistona australis
Rat Island 56, 63
recycling *see* waste management
refrigeration 126
rehabilitation 94, 98–9
    revegetation cycle 95
research station 72
Rhizophora stylosa 81
Roe, Reginald 70, 72
Roe's Kamp 70, 77, 77
Rosebud 24, 24, 26, 30, 35, 45
rubbish compactor 108, 130, 132
Runaway Bay 49, 56

sack fungi 81
salt marshes 98
Salter, Lindy 57
sand dunes 45, 46–7, 61, 99, 150, 188–9
    erosion 71
    rehabilitating 72, 99, 136–7
sandfly bush 94
sandmining 70, 71, 71–2, 99, 120
    prevents development 70, 70
Scottish Prince 66, 69
sedge 61, 98, 99, 179
sewage treatment 130, 132, 132–3, 133

shield bug 106
shipwrecks 66, 69
Sinclair Knight Merz 81
Small, Bruce 44
Smith, David 82
snake, brown tree 107
soils 63
    see also acid sulfate soils
Solanum aviculare 60
solar power 88, 127
    for hot water 126, 165
    light traps 135
soldier crabs 23, 84–5, 119
solid waste *see* rubbish compactor
South Stradbroke Island 19, 39, 56, 57, 57–77
    history 57–77
    Pacific Island Club site 44–5
    recreational value 69, 69, 77
    separates from North Stradbroke 62, 62, 69
    site 49
    see also ocean beach
South Stradbroke Island Resort 71
Southport Seaway 72, 77
Spa Island 140, 150, 151, 154, 155, 156–7, 159, 184–5
Spa Island Cafe 155
spinifex, beach 58, 61, 98, 99, 136–7, 188–9
Spinifex sericeus 61, 98, 136–7, 188–9
spoonbill, royal 113
Sports 156
Sprint Track 124, 124
staff *see* Couran Cove Resort
Steeley, Colin 70
Stielow, Henry 50
stilts, black-winged 176–7
surf beach *see* ocean beach
Surf Club restaurant 158
Surfers Paradise 48, 70
Surfing Recreation Reserve 77
swamp oak 41

terns 22
threatened species 88
timber cutting 99
Tipplers 71
Todiramphus sancta 108
tree ferns 17
tree frog, graceful 1, 81
tree snake, brown 107
Tremewen, Ian 165
Trichoglossus haematodus 57
Trott, David 140
Tuesley family 69

UV treatment unit 130, 133

Vacuum Sewer System 132
Varanus varius 110–11
vermiculture 108, 130, 131, 131, 132, 133
violet, native 94

wallaby, agile 4, 19, 45, 96–7, 109, 169
Walker, Evan 50

waste management 119, 130, 130–3, 131
    using waste heat 127
water lily, giant 169
water management 119, 120–1
    Nanofiltration 121
weed control 89, 94, 98–9
Welsby, Thomas 63, 66, 69
wetlands 113
    paperbark 74–5
    pest control in 134
    salt marshes 98
    see also mangroves, Melaleuca swamp
Wilderness Lodges 154
wind power 127, 127
worm farm *see* vermiculture

For the chapter *The Island and its History* (pages 56–79)

REFERENCES
Brisbane Courier, 21.7.1880; 21.5.1898.
Courier Mail, 25.5.1968.
Hardie, Jean *Southport*. (Typescript, John Oxley Library)
Logan and Albert Bulletin, 6.3.1897.
Meston, A. 1865, 'Moreton Bay and Islands' in *Handbook of Excursions of the Australian Association for the Advancement of Science*, Pole, Outridge & Co, Brisbane.
Neal, R. & Stock, E. 1986, 'Pleistocene Occupation in the South-eastern Queensland Coastal Region', *Nature*, 323, 16 October.
Ponosov, V. V. 1964, *Results of an Archaeological Survey of the Southern Region of Moreton Bay and of Moreton Island*, University of Queensland Press, Brisbane.
Roe, Charles *A History of Roe's Kamp*. (Typescript, John Oxley Library)
Smith, Glen 1882, 'What happened to the Queensland Oyster Industry'. Reprint from *Australian Fisheries*, March.
Thompson, A. K. (ed.) 1967, *The Collected Works of Thomas Welsby*, vols I and II, Jacaranda Press, Brisbane.

INTERVIEWS
Tom Dalton, Hooker-Rex, Sydney.
Graham Dillon, 'Kalwun', Nerang.
Bob Latter, Couran.
Norm Medland, Southport.
Lachie Tuesley, Labrador.

Live the Dream • Never say Never

... if you can fill the unforgiving minute with sixty seconds worth of distance run...
RUDYARD KIPLING